Feminine Voices

True Stories by Women Transforming Leadership

Heal My Voice, Inc
Santa Monica, California

Feminine Voices: True Stories by Women Transforming Leadership

Published by:
Heal My Voice, Inc
Andrea Hylen
Santa Monica, CA 90401
www.healmyvoice.org

ISBN-13: 978-0692313664 (Heal My Voice)
ISBN-10: 0692313664

Editor: Andrea Hylen
Cover design by Karen Brand

Printed in the United States of America

A portion of the proceeds from the sale of this book will be donated to further the non-profit work of Heal My Voice.

Dedication

This book is dedicated to the women who came before us who had the courage and willingness to stand up and use their voices, to lay a path for us to follow and to the women who have picked up the baton to run the next part of the race.

We see you.

Your Voice Matters.

Blessing

Rev. Jamie Dee Fisher

Our deepest fear is not that we are inadequate. Our deepest fear is that we are powerful beyond measure. It is our light, not our darkness that frightens us. We ask ourselves, who am I to be brilliant, gorgeous, talented and fabulous? Actually, who are you not to be? ~ Marianne Williamson

These words by Marianne Williamson have always been one of the most inspiring quotes I've ever heard. It takes incredible courage to stand in your light without shame, or fear, or pride.

Feminine leadership is an often-misunderstood concept, much like feminism. Too many for too long have thought of it as an "us versus them" kind of mentality. That in order for women to rise, men had to fall. This could not be further from the truth. These women who have courageously stepped forward into their light to share their stories understand that true feminine leadership can only come about by honoring both the divine feminine AND the divine masculine within themselves. They have found the balance. They have learned that there is immense strength in showing your tenderness, your compassion, and your ability to nurture yourself as well as others. Feminine Leadership is not soft, nor weak, nor fleeting ~ no, feminine leadership takes tremendous courage, strength and conviction to believe that there is a better way ~ a way of peace, of love, of compassion, of tenderness, of equality for all.

We are blessed by the courage of these women. Through their stories, we are inspired to live our lives more fully, more completely, more openly, more authentically. These women have proven that their lives have been profoundly blessed, despite the otherwise outward appearances of their trials and tribulations. They have heard their calling, and they have answered, proving that the power of their feminine strength can be manifested in ways both grand and intimate.

May you, the reader, be blessed with the inspiration found among these pages so that you may go forward in your own life and find the strength to live it as deeply and authentically as the authors.

May love, compassion and wisdom continue to bless the lives of these women and all whom they touch.

In gratitude and appreciation,
Rev. Jamie Dee Fisher

Jamie Dee is blessed to be a mom to her amazing son, Logan who provides endless laughter, light and inspiration. She is a relationship communication educator, coach, author, speaker and workshop leader. Jamie is a non-denominational minister who loves creating beautiful, customized vows & performing wedding ceremonies. As a dual doctoral candidate in psychology & theology, and years of being a dedicated Heart-Centered Metaphysician, Jamie provides a positive, nurturing support system that allows her clients to grow & reach their full potential. Jamie is a Life Coach who offers extensive Premarital Counseling & Marriage Enrichment packages as well as gentle guidance on how to have a graceful divorce & move forward with life through her Divorce Coaching program and in her soon to be released book, "A Graceful Divorce; Learning How to Communicate with Integrity, Respect & Honor".

You can reach Jamie at the following:
www.A-Passionate-Life.com
JamieDee@consultant.com,
www.facebook.com/JamieDee.APassionateLife

TABLE OF CONTENTS

Part One: I AM Authentic

Part Four: I AM Prepared

Sponsors: 247

Lisa Hall

Mary K. Baxter
Cassandra Herbert
Ellen Koronet
Marie Ek Lipanovska
Monisha Mittal
Karen Porter
Amber Scott
Jamie Dee Schiffer
Beth Terrence
Kathleen Nelson Troyer

FOREWORD

Mary K. Baxter

I was raised to lead, cultivated by a family and a community who held me to a high standard of leadership: Director of my Odyssey of the Mind team in Middle School, lead actress in theatre productions, President of Future Business Leaders of America in High School, and President of Alpha Psi Omega, a National Honors Theatre Fraternity in College. I led teams in class projects, I organized events before I held higher positions in extra curricular activities, and I coordinated collaborations between organizations to propel new projects into being. I was born to lead.

Throughout my young life, I would hear snippets of, *"Don't be so bossy; why do you always have to be in control?"* My ideas, my vision of the big picture shut down by the notion that by thinking big I was somehow making others feel small. It confused me, briefly, but I was raised in a household where I was encouraged to think bigger and work harder, so it never stopped me in my tracks.

Eight years ago, I collaborated with a fellow theatre artist to begin a new theatre company. We had this crazy idea to bring actors to disenfranchised communities to work with kids and teach them storytelling skills. Together we wrote a business plan, built a website, made a budget, auditioned actors and organized a project for a group to travel to

Zimbabwe. We heard a lot of, "what are you thinking, why would you do this, how is this possible." But, the vision was so big and our mission was so clear that it just couldn't stop us from pushing forward. Even a glitch at the passport office, which had me on an overnight bus from NYC to Baltimore and down to DC to wait in the passport line for 12 hours on the day of my flight didn't stop me from getting documents faxed to me, changing my flight from NY to DC and meeting my team on our layover in London.

We arrived in Harare, and there we were, ready to take action. We had our team with everything organized to a "T." The financial crisis in Zimbabwe was a challenge and one that I took on with gusto. We could only withdraw 1.5 Million Zimbabwe Dollars per day from the bank (this translated to about 12 US Dollars.) Most of our lodging was free, and we were able to use the card at the grocery store and some restaurants to buy food. Problems managed.

Our only dilemma was getting petrol for our host's car. He was driving us from community to community, so we were using fuel fast, and there were not only shortages of petrol at the station, but when they would get a delivery there were long lines at the station- and this was during our scheduled theatre classes. We had to come up with an alternate plan.

The team was invited to dinner at the home of the community leader. After we ate, the women went into the kitchen to clean up and the team members went with them. My partner and I stayed with the community leaders to discuss a plan for the petrol.

Writing this foreword, until this moment, I didn't think it was relevant to share with you that my theatre partner is a man. Until this moment, I didn't think it was relevant to share that I am a woman. And that evening, until that moment after dinner, I don't think I had realized that I was a little girl in a room full of middle-aged male community leaders.

I don't remember the words that were said in this meeting, and I don't want to falsify the event with made up words. All I can speak to is how I felt. I felt small. I felt like my voice didn't matter. I felt like I would ask a question and the response would be directed at my male partner. I felt out of place. I felt that my ideas were irrelevant. I felt like I didn't belong, that I should be in the kitchen cleaning dishes, like my contribution to the conversation was null.

What I do remember is that I contributed to the solution. I gave our host cash and he, graciously, waited in line for hours to fill up the tank, as well as a few barrels of petrol that we were able to access throughout our trip. We gifted him the remainder when we left.

Although my voice is ever so strong, and my business partner- then boyfriend, now husband- would argue that my opinions are as feisty as ever, it did take me a while to regain my confidence to lead in these settings again. I still occasionally have to step back and look at the larger picture to see what others have seen in me my whole life, I am a leader.

This is why this book is relevant. The eighteen authors in this book all have their own unique experience of gaining and reclaiming their voice of leadership. Some of them are in the first stage of leadership, still doubting if the term "leader" applies to them, while others have been confidently leading for years.

As you experience the stories in this book, my hope is that it will spark, or rekindle, the voice of leadership in your own life. Our voices matter, and as we strengthen our voices we lift up everyone around us.

Your voice matters too.

Mary K. Baxter co-founded Dramatic Adventure Theatre in 2006, only months after completing her BA. She works as a consulting non-profit and arts administrator for companies in NYC and beyond. In addition to being a Heal My Voice author, Mary K serves as a Board Member, helping to further the mission of empowering women and girls to reclaim their voices and step into greater leadership. As a daughter, sister, mother and friend, Mary K has surrounded herself with powerful women, but it is in her partnership with her husband and their theatre company that she has found the true strength of her feminine voice.
www.dramaticadventure.com

Introduction

Andrea Hylen

Founder of Heal My Voice

Feminine Leadership.

Is leadership different for women than men? Is it time for women to find new, more authentic ways of leading? Can women influence men to lead differently?

Every Heal My Voice book project consists of an intention around a topic focus for the stories. The intention for this project was for each woman to explore and examine her experiences with leadership, to look at past experiences, to dissect each situation, to explore her authentic expression and style and to discover what it means to be a woman leader in 2014.

We began by reflecting on a question: *What are some qualities of Feminine Leadership?*

The list included the following: Integrity, Authentic Heart, Compassion, Flow, Being, Love, Inner Strength, Connecting, Listening, Holding the Space, Nurturing, Presence, Vulnerability, Strength, Honoring Myself and Others, Creativity, Courage, Receiving, Connected with the

Earth, Allowing, Spiritual, Universal, and Intuitive.

Our conversations evolved with the exploration of feminine and masculine leadership and new models of organizational structures. We shared videos, articles and stories while we listened to TEDtalks about leaning in and pushing back, articles that included the examination of *Changing Corporate Culture to Enable Women's Success* and *Vulnerability as Power*. We independently took other classes with words in the titles like priestess, power, sensuality, Mother Mary, feminine process, the red tent, the passion test, the desire map and untamed you.

One of the authors, Monisha Mittal, saw a SIGN in the first month of the program and posted it in the group: *Good things are happening: New entrance under construction*. The words "under construction" were a good description of what each of us took on as we deconstructed then reconstructed who we are as leaders now.

I learned a lot about myself as a leader. By the time the leadership project was beginning to form, I made the hard decision to end a collaborative initiative to have a co-leader in this project and instead moved forward to lead it on my own. In order to do that I had to let go of being the nice girl and make a decision I felt was best for the project and Heal My Voice as a whole. I learned *what is not collaboration* and I learned *why the collaboration broke down*. The process of that was complex and will be a story for another day.

The experience of *holding space* for the women in this group stretched me as a leader and to be blunt, I had a year in my personal life where my *"people pleasing and nice girl acquiescing"* style of community building got her ass kicked out the door. I have learned how to artfully penetrate, to hold more discomfort in my body when someone tries to control me or reacts with anger or temper tantrums, to ask for what I want and to say the things out loud that I see before others see them even when it makes other people uncomfortable.

There was a period of four months towards the end of the project when the group was so quiet, I wondered if any of our stories would ever be completed. Instead of standing on the stage, each of us had a deeper period of reflection and inner work needed for the next step in leadership to emerge.

And then something shifted. As I arrived in Sweden for a five-week work retreat with Marie Ek Lipanovska, the founder of Heal My Voice Sweden, I could feel something bubbling in the group. The energy was rising again.

There was an expansion of the "bridge" between Sweden and the United States and our global connection. I presented a workshop to an international audience in person for the first time. And then I intuitively knew the next steps and took inspired action. It was time to challenge the women to begin a "Game" to write and complete our stories. I set a time period and took daily action with information, writing prompts, guidance and deadlines. The "masculine" energy welled up out of the "feminine."

The Game:

Goal: To complete our stories in 30 days.
Time period: August 25 - September 25, 2014

*Write 15-30 minutes every day.
*Community Call Scheduled every Tues for support
*Find at least one person in the group and tell them your story.
*Gentle reading process
*Story is 1500-2000 words

Of the 22 women in the group, 18 women completed stories. (And one woman wrote a second story.)

The women in this book are a reflection of the vision of Heal My Voice. They are strong, inspiring, powerful everyday, extraordinary women who want to make a difference in the world, who see possibilities where others have lost hope, who have a voice filled with ideas, visions and who are willing to do the work. These women made a commitment to go inward, to discover their unique gifts, to "clean house" where an old style of leading was holding them back and now they are ready to share their journey with you.

They had the courage to be vulnerable and transparent, allow themselves to unravel their style of leadership, look at what was working and let go of what was not working. The stories are a reflection of their lives, their experiences and the deep inner transformation they experienced this year.

One of the inspirations for this book came from a quote by *His Holiness the Dalai Lama, at the Peace Summit in Vancouver, 2011.*

"The world will be saved by the western woman," ~ His Holiness the Dalai Lama, at the Peace Summit in Vancouver, 2011.

The eighteen women authors in this book give you a glimpse of what it looks like when the western woman explores and discovers herself as a leader. The women share stories of transforming their leadership styles in work, parenting, health care, recovery and love. They challenged themselves to become more visible, to share their unique gifts, to offer new ideas, to heal old wounds and to take inspired action. Their stories demonstrate what is possible when Western women take their place as leaders in the world.

We hope that by reading their stories, you will discover more about yourself and step into greater leadership in your life.

Andrea Hylen *believes in the power of a woman's voice to usher in a new world. She is the founder of Heal My Voice, a Minister of Spiritual Peacemaking, a Writing and Transition Coach and Orgasmic Meditation teacher. Andrea has discovered her unique gifts while parenting three daughters and learning to live life fully after the deaths of her brother, son and husband. She is currently living out of a suitcase following her intuition as she collaborates with women and men in organizations and travels around the world speaking, teaching and leading workshops. Her passion is authentically living life and supporting others in doing the same. To connect with Andrea and learn about current projects go to: www.andreahylen.com and **www.healmyvoice.org**.*

Part One

I Am Visible

"The authentic self is the soul made visible "

-Sarah Ban Breathnach

Story One

My Authentic Life

Lisa Hall

"Don't be so bossy," she said sharply and I immediately lowered my head and shrank inside making myself small. I was only seven and felt confused, embarrassed and ashamed by my mother's scolding. My excitement to teach my friend what I knew about a game was squashed, my brightness dimmed. This is one of many memories I have of my mother criticizing me; of trying to make sure I was "appropriate" in public. Like so many suppressed women of her generation, she had a knack for doing this with a look—you know the "evil eye" or overtly with a sharp tongue. I was naturally an optimistic, fun-loving, effervescent child with an incredibly sensitive heart. Because of my deep sensitivity, I took in all my mother's criticisms and became extremely self-conscious and worried about what others thought of me.

Over time I began to question myself. Can I stand the sound of my own voice? Is it ok for me to use it? To speak?

To sing? What if I say things they don't want to hear or things they don't like? What if they don't like the way I sound? What if they don't like me? All of these questions derived from fear bump up against my deep need to communicate; to share higher truths; philosophical ideas; psychological musings.

I have always worked in a predominantly female environment as a teacher and counselor. During group meetings with women I was often sought out to share ideas or experiences and *seemed to be respected* for my expertise. After a period of time though certain interactions led me to feel rejected and judged as arrogant for the actual sharing. I kept trying to fit in and gain acceptance. I automatically had to make myself small and not stand out. After all I had learned to be "appropriate" in public. I was so self-conscious and assumed that there was something wrong with me. I thought I was deeply flawed and less than and that is why I felt and was so rejected. I wish I had understood then that often these other women were wounded too, feeling jealous or inadequate themselves. The self-consciousness that led me to shrink and reject myself coupled with the belief I should give way to the needs of others first grew out of many experiences in my childhood where I never felt like I could take up my rightful space here on the planet. Not only did I not consider my needs, I didn't even know I had them. I couldn't lead myself if I didn't know myself at this fundamental level.

In late 2012 on a group trip to Morocco, the concept of leadership came to the forefront of my mind. I began to contemplate, examine and review who I was as a leader. In that contemplation, I identified a couple of wounds around leadership. One wound occurred when I was a young professional and the other involved the internalized self-critical voice that developed over time during my childhood.

One specific incident as a young professional had a powerful impact on me. During the first three months as a counselor at an in-home therapy program I felt so overwhelmed and incompetent. I had been a teacher for eight years and although I was excited to begin my new career I was unprepared for the feelings of inadequacy that would pervade my new experience. Through tears I told my supervisor, Julie, that I didn't know what made me think I could be a therapist. She calmly and convincingly said, "You are the most natural therapist I have ever met who has had no experience. You will get it. It takes time." She believed in me and supported me and within 6 months I began to shine. My innate understanding of what was needed for healing emerged. I was asked to share my insights and interventions at staff meetings and I became a "go-to" person for clinical support on the team. I was supported to reach my goal, to become a Licensed Professional Counselor.

I became friends with my fellow clinicians and was really happy to be part of a team. Julie left the agency and a friend and fellow clinician on our staff was promoted to the supervisory position. She continued to support and encourage my leadership among the team of counselors. Once again I found myself in a leadership position, able to share the things that excited me. The natural teacher in me gets very enthusiastic and excited when people wake up to some self-understanding and make a change that improves their quality of life. It has always been true about me, a part of my essence.

I worked in an intensive in-home therapy program funded by Medicaid. We provided services to families where kids were at risk from being removed from their home or coming back into the family after an out of home placement.

These were families who had many holes in their bucket. It was often heartbreaking, sometimes maddening, always intense and mostly rewarding. I feel certain that my time there significantly deepened my understanding of the issues people face and shaped my therapeutic skills. I became more confident as a young professional working with these children and families. It was during my one-on-one weekly supervision meetings that I was encouraged to share my insights and interventions on specific cases with the staff in order to teach others about the therapeutic process. I felt affirmed in my decision to become a therapist and was happy to be fulfilling what I believe to be my life purpose. After two years working as a clinician and receiving supervision I became a Licensed Professional Counselor.

Then it happened. I was called into **the** meeting. I didn't know what was about to hit me but there were about 9 or 10 of us at the table and I was in the "hot seat". My friend turned supervisor decided to hold an "intervention". I'm sure there may have been some feedback that I could have used if it had been delivered constructively. However this intervention was designed so that everyone (all women by the way) could tell me what they each didn't like about me and essentially how I was "too big". It appeared as though the goal of my supervisor was to break me, humiliate me, and put me in my place. It was shocking and I was frozen with fear. I wanted to leave the room but I literally could not move. I listened as one by one my colleagues shared their negative opinions of me. Eventually I broke down and cried. I left the meeting stunned and shaken to my core. I was so confused. I had been encouraged to share, to teach, to shine. I searched for answers as I reviewed various scenarios and conversations in my mind for what I did wrong. There had been no direction in any one-on-one meetings with my supervisor that I needed to do things differently. Although I could find no indication I still blamed myself and I really lost trust in everything—other people and most importantly myself. I sobbed for a couple of days. I felt so alone as I processed the pain. I remember having a conscious thought: Other people give you power, other people take your power away. Even though I had opened a private practice with a seasoned group of clinicians, I still needed the In-Home job. So I hid my pain and I held my head high and continued to treat families in the best way I could.

I was deeply hurt on so many levels as a result of that meeting. I questioned my abilities as a clinician. I questioned what I thought I knew about myself. I questioned my perceptions about relationships, the one with my supervisor as well as the ones with my "friends" / colleagues. I did understand that many of my colleagues didn't feel they had a choice in the meeting. They wouldn't go against our supervisor otherwise they could find themselves in my position—the "hot seat". And yet some of my colleagues seemed to revel in their opportunity to tear me down. It felt like a "witch-hunt". The one in power, the "leader", led the others to shun.

This experience sent me into hiding. I worked and saw clients and brought my best work forward but I clammed up in groups. The program closed within 3 months and we were all out of a job because our supervisor had neglected her duties to the program at large. I have come to realize now that poor boundaries at this work place and feelings of jealousy as well as judgment and competition were at play in this scenario. I was simply being myself and doing what came naturally to me so I didn't really see my gifts and abilities as special. I therefore couldn't understand why anyone would feel jealous of me at that time. It made no sense in my mind. I thought everyone was of value and so I didn't understand the competition piece either. While this was truly the most painful and significant of my experiences of being squashed and shut down, there were other group experiences where I felt I should be small as well.

While "hiding" was a painful choice in response to these situations, it also led me on a path to further deepen my self-understanding and self-healing. It was in this process of healing the painful belief, "I didn't have a right to take up space" that I realized it was the deepest wound of all. Feeling like I couldn't express my own thoughts and opinions without approval and validation led to the pain I experienced in the group settings where I felt misunderstood and rejected. In addition, my constant replay of the internalized version of my mother's critical voice inside my head continued to repeat negative patterns. I focused on my shortcomings and amplified my own feelings of inadequacy. In order to really heal the pain and gain wisdom I went inward to explore the many experiences in which I believed this. I challenged these beliefs and began to replace them with healthier perceptions.

The process was sometimes messy and often uncomfortable. I really came to know and understand who I really am by immersing myself in the study of "Me". I found supportive facilitators on this journey that encouraged me to grow and heal. I aligned with all of the courage I could muster to heal the dark shadowy places where the pain resided. Reclaiming the power I lost to that pain allowed me to solidify my core sense of self, step into my inner authority and express more of my authentic self. I take up my rightful space on the planet now. Not more, not less, just what is mine. I now lead myself daily in every way. I listen to my intuitive voice, the voice that directs me to my highest and best good in any given moment. While I can enjoy being in groups, I don't let the group define me. I am learning to share my thoughts and wisdom without attachment to the outcome. I write, speak, and sing more freely now. People can take what they like and leave the rest. I've come to believe that we are all meant to lead ourselves and then leading others follows naturally. Mastering this is key. I own my Presence. I own my Light. I am so grateful for the journey that has led me to be, claim and express my Authentic Self!

Lisa Hall is a Licensed Professional Counselor, Coach and Catalyst for healing and growth. As a modern day mystic, Lisa integrates perceptions from the metaphysical realm into her daily life and work. Using a penetrating focus coupled with deep compassion, Lisa assists her clients to become aware of limiting beliefs and repeating negative patterns. With clarity and wisdom, Lisa helps to shift these limiting perceptions opening pathways of Light so people can deepen into their core, discover their truth, claim their personal power and express more of their Soul Essence. Lisa lives with her beloved husband David in Fulton, MD. In addition to her work she enjoys singing, photography and practices yoga.

For more information about Lisa's work please visit
www.dynamicalternatives.com.

Story Two

My Quiet Power

Nancy Nicholson Kobel

"Becoming a leader is synonymous with becoming yourself. It is precisely that simple, and it is also that difficult." ~Warren Bennis

Reclaiming my feminine power. Before I started writing this story, I didn't even know it was missing or that I kept giving it away. It sat quietly on the shelf, appearing every once in a while but never fully developed.

I showed up in this world with a quiet power, an internal strength. I was influenced adversely at an early age by the voices outside of me – the grownups; those that labeled me as shy, as quiet, as "in my shell", as if there was something inherently "wrong" with me. That 'who' I was and 'how' I showed up in this world with this quiet power was not OK. That quiet was not power. That quiet was weak. And that quiet was most definitely not found in leadership roles. This was the birth of a limiting belief: "I am not a leader!" So I placed my power on a shelf only tapping into it rarely. But this power included more, it wasn't just my quiet power that was on a shelf, my feminine power sat right next to it. The belief that both quiet and feminine had less value was reinforced in a world that praised extroversion and masculine traits.

When my quiet power showed up as leadership – it was fierce, yet it was calm and confident, based on a combination of internal knowing backed with data communicated with passion. It didn't show up nearly enough…until I truly claimed it and integrated it into my life.

Third grade: Quiet, kind, introspective and intelligent. I sat in Mrs. Carter's third grade class. The walls were blue cinder block, a statue of St. Therese was just above the chalkboards. Bulletin boards were on each side of the chalkboards, decorated for the seasons. My favorite was the one next to the door. This was the one where we got our name placed on the board once we mastered our multiplication tables. Waiting for my turn, my turn to shine, to ace the multiplication tables…. 8, 16, 24… 56, 64, …..88, 96. Success! First to know it, name up on the board, accomplishment and praise!

Eighth grade, captain of the cheerleading squad and valedictorian of my class, but I'm not a leader….

Early 1980's: My brains had me in all honors classes and excelling in math and science –the seeds were planted early to pursue a degree in engineering. Teamed with determination, I graduated with an Aerospace Engineering degree. After college, I worked as a thermal engineer on some amazing programs with equally amazing and collaborative teams for NASA. I was surrounded by men, worked with men, and sometimes I was the only woman present. I became comfortable in the masculine energy. It was fun, easy going, goal oriented and non-judgmental.

I love to learn and after a few years, I wanted to expand beyond the engineering. I tried for task leads and other positions. I didn't get them… oh yeah, I wasn't a leader. I felt like a caged bird whose wings were about to be clipped if I didn't take conscious action. The thought of looking forward and seeing myself as a thermal engineer 20-30 years down the road scared me. So I did the research, determined my next steps and followed my heart. A Masters degree in Instructional Design and a career change into Training and Development.

With encouragement from my peers, I shared my career path with the leaders of the organization. By the time I graduated, I transitioned into a new role in Human Resources and embraced the learning before me. My new focus was primarily on the management development of engineers.

More change was coming. The beginning of 2006 began with a dark night of the soul, a cancer diagnosis and a waking up to my spiritual insight. I was deep in motherhood with two small children, working part-time, and trying to hold it all together. Despite being surrounded by friends and family, I felt very much alone on my spiritual journey, having no one to truly share it with. As a true engineer, I went into problem solving mode. What was I going to do? I was in 'overwhelm', and it was time to reconnect with my heart. I learned about forgiveness and unconditional love and was reminded of my intuitive gifts. I was remembering things I had forgotten. Tears flowed daily. Emotions I hadn't felt in years enveloped me, as I reclaimed my strong yet gentle heart. The walls around it had collapsed. It was now open and in awe of the power of love. I was not shutting it down again, the cost was way too high.

As the year came to a close, I received another gift. With my gentle heart wide open, a blast of energy shot up and down my spine. There was so much energy pulsing through my body, it felt as if there was enough power to light up the county I was in, if not the entire state of Maryland and even possibly New York City. I had no words yet I intuitively knew -- it was the secret to healing the world's problems. The feminine energy in complete balance with the masculine energy – just a drop could bring about world peace. I knew it in my bones. I sensed it and I was forever changed.

The feminine energy lay dormant since I was a child. It was suppressed so the masculine energy could accomplish, and succeed in a masculine world. After this surge of energy, I couldn't speak for days. My logical brain tried to make sense of my experience (to no avail) and I was grateful for Google so I could confirm I wasn't crazy. In true introvert fashion, I read, I learned and I researched. I had access to my feminine energy. This was a beginning. It would take years to fully claim it as mine and integrate it with the masculine.

While I learned more, my career in learning and development continued. I loved leadership development, facilitating classes, and coaching employees. I loved anything talent management related especially helping others develop and succeed! While my career was expanding, I began to expand my circles outside of work, finding like-minded women where I could show up completely as myself, as a woman, embracing my soul's journey without judgment.

*2009: My mentor: "You have a delicate heart, not weak, but strong and gentle." I let the words seep in, trying to understand.

*2011: A manager: "I can just sit in your office and go from chaos to calm. I don't know what it is."

*2013: A coach: "I can just stand next to you, in your presence and not say a word. I could stand here all day."

It was my presence that was the gift, my quiet, gentle, powerful heart that helped those around me. Finally, I got it. I didn't have to be loud, be like someone else, talk non-stop, and I didn't have to hide. This was one of the gifts that truly complemented my coaching. I didn't have to change it to fit in. I just had to own it.

2013 was a year of endings, my marriage was officially over, the company I had been with for almost 23 years was no longer aligned with who I was and the employment ended. The journey I started to become a certified professional coach a year earlier was complete. I also continued to nurture my connections with women and became a published author in an anthology book with 22 amazing women. The year leading up to these endings was a year of motion, a lot of doing. I finally had an opportunity to just be. I discovered I had more work to do and the year ahead was not short on the challenges and lessons I needed to learn. Despite enjoying the feminine energy of just Being for a few months, my energy was still split; the masculine and feminine were still not integrated.

At the top of the list was loving myself, completely and unconditionally,. To learn how to stop worrying about what others thought or said about me behind my back, asking for help and learning how to receive graciously. I have been learning how to set healthy boundaries and communicate those boundaries, keeping walls down while protecting my power and my heart. I had to take action and let go of the outcome, recognizing others had their lessons to learn also. Sometimes it felt as if I was holding the spoon, and someone else was stirring the pot. Something as simple as setting up a carpool turned into a challenge, I was asking for help, yet it took over a month of consistent action, trying different things, having conversations and finally walking down a different road.

Stepping into leadership can be scary. It can have you shaking in your shoes. It opens you up to judgment by others, slander, and gossip. It puts you in a place of vulnerability where the eyes are on you and the perception of you is based on their experiences, their journey, and their path. It also allows you to make a difference in the lives of those that hear what they need to hear.

I had two opportunities to speak in October of 2013, one at a conference with all women, an amazing experience of connection. The other opportunity was both men and women in a professional environment.

I was standing on the stage in front of about 100 people. I felt nervous and vulnerable. Would they hear me? The message I wanted to convey. Would they get it and take it to heart? I knew not all would. After I walked off the stage, I received positive feedback from several in attendance.

After the meeting, I was standing among a number of men who were talking. One made a sarcastic comment about my presentation, while another implied I would let such a comment make me second-guess myself. I had no words and was a bit in shock. I suppressed my emotions for the moment and took care of the tasks at hand. When I was sitting back at my computer, I couldn't concentrate, the tears where coming and I was not going to be able to stop them. I tried to make it to the bathroom without anyone noticing, I was unsuccessful and grateful for the two compassionate individuals who caught me. Vulnerability is difficult, being open to attack and judgment is hard but as a leader, it is part of the deal. The release was powerful and needed. Crying, for me, is a welcome emotion that provides a release. I spent too many years suppressing and keeping in my emotions. Tears aren't a sign of weakness. They are a sign of being human.

The deadline for the completion of this story was fast approaching and I was stuck, something else was needed. I kept trying to write but couldn't seem to bring it together. I sat on my deck, taking in my surroundings, the lush green grass, the trees, the birds chirping, when the tears started to flow. I welcomed them. The tears weren't coming from a place of despair but a place of release. Releasing the wounds from the past, the memories of the past, the fear and recognizing I am so much more than I ever thought I was. That the divine feminine power that was released back in 2006 wasn't external to me, it was internal. I wasn't going to get it through approval or love from others. It was within me all along.

As I reflect back on my life and my experiences, attributes like quiet or loud, introverted or extroverted have nothing to do with leadership. It is how we show up authentically and present. So much feminine power has been suppressed, diminished in not just me but many girls and women around me. We don't know our own power and we haven't lived in environments where we were encouraged to be powerful in a feminine way. We are worthy of receiving great love and the first step is unconditional self-love. Not only loving ourselves, but also loving the women around us and seeing their beauty even when they do not see it themselves. We have some healing to do if we are to truly transform the world into a better place.

And as we heal we can help the men in our lives to embrace their power. We need to love and accept them and communicate in a way they can hear us. We need to ask them for their help in bringing balance together. We can't do it without them, just as we can't change the world hanging out in just masculine energy or just feminine energy. We need both in balance to truly transform the world. We have work to do. Are you in?

I know I am.

Nancy Nicholson Kobel is a transformational life and leadership coach, professionally trained and accredited through the International Coach Federation (ICF). Nancy is founder of Leader Inspired, LLC. She works from her heart center, with both men and women, providing the tools and an environment that gets to the core of what is holding her clients back from having the success and joy they truly desire in life and work. This is her second story for Heal My Voice and is grateful to be part of the amazing work this organization is providing. Nancy lives in Maryland with her two teens and looks forward connecting and helping to transform the world. Nancy can be contacted at info@leaderinspired.com and www.leaderinspired.com

Story Three

Stepping In

Nukhet Govdeli Hendricks

As I sat there and watched her cry, I felt the anxiety beginning to build up inside me. Her tears were big; so big that I could see my own reflection in them as they were rolling down her cheeks. Something was wrong! Something was **terribly** wrong. My staff person was crying so hard and so soulfully that my heart was breaking all the while realizing that something had to change; my leadership style was not working and I was completely clueless as to what I was doing to bring the tears.

In my twenties, while living in Turkey, I never thought much about leadership, let alone female leadership. I was able to do anything and everything I wanted professionally while making a very good living. Honestly, female leadership was not even a concept I was familiar with at that time, let alone knew what it was all about. All I knew was, being a woman did not stop me from doing anything I wanted to do.

Then I moved to the United States in 1987. All of a sudden I was hearing about leadership but what I was hearing was not exactly about female leadership. The message I was receiving was all about "removing" the female from leadership. I remember reading so many headlines and articles in women's magazines about how to survive in a man's world. All articles advised women to: "wear suits, in black, navy or gray"; "dress conservatively"; "do not use words like 'I feel' because they are not power words"; "be like one of the guys". Basically, women were being advised to forget about the fact that they were women. These points of view left me completely perplexed because I had never been told that I should be like a man if I wanted to succeed in a man's world. On top of everything else, the trainings I was attending were emphasizing the hierarchical, coercive, authoritative, "do as I tell you" model more and more. (By the way... I did a quick search for leadership books on Amazon as I was writing my story. The first 24 books on leadership that came up on the list only had **one book** that was written by a female!)

I got my first leadership job in 1997. And the first time I spoke up to a man to express my point of view which contradicted his point of view, he looked me in the eyes and said "You are too strong for a woman!"

I was completely baffled! How could I possibly be too strong for a woman? Were there degrees of strength? And a woman can only have a certain degree of strength? I couldn't even comprehend what had just happened. However, this interaction pretty much set the tone for my leadership. Be strong no matter what even if it meant being "too strong for a woman"! Don't let them see you sweat! Produce results! Make it happen! These became the values I have been embodying and practicing in my leadership which eventually brought me to my office where I was sitting, watching my staff person cry, all the while crumbling inside knowing something had gone terribly wrong.

This all happened on a Friday night. I had the entire weekend to stew over this, wondering what went wrong. It didn't matter how hard I tried not to look at the obvious, pretending it wasn't there. In the end, all the proverbial fingers were still pointing at me. At the end of the weekend, I was certain that I had to do something. I had to go on a major inner leadership overhaul. The only thing I knew that would help me at this point was to work with a leadership coach. The irony was I was the graduate of a rather reputable life-coaching program and I didn't have the faintest idea how to coach myself at this point let alone change what was happening at work.

I started the process of interviewing a few leadership coaches who were incidentally all females. I was confident that I was going to find a leadership coach who was willing to work with me on my leadership skills before we even worried about my staff person. Interestingly, the first three coaches I interviewed told me that maybe I just simply had to let go of the staff person because she may not be suitable for the job. I was stumped and disappointed because I knew the staff person was qualified for the job. I had no desire to fire her. First I had to figure out what on earth was wrong with my leadership style considering she was not the first staff member to cry.

Then I remembered my mentor coach who coached me when I was going through my life coaching training and whom I absolutely adored. I sought her out and found out that she was now an executive leadership coach. I knew that was my answer from the divine. This was the first time I realized that this was all divinely ordered and the angels were watching over me.

We started coaching and during one of the sessions, she asked: "How do you use your gift of intuition in your leadership?"

I was completely taken back. "I don't use my gift of intuition in my leadership" I said. I added "I actually leave that part of me at home; I put my 'executive director' hat on and go to work. I cannot possibly be emotional or intuitive nor do things from the heart at work. I have to be the strong one, not the emotional one".

Silence...

Then she asked "How can you possibly lead effectively and lovingly if you leave your heart and essence at home?"

I was stunned. For the first time in my life, I was hearing the words "heart and lead" used within the same sentence. What I realized about my own leadership style literally brought me down to my knees. I was leading my organization and staff while leaving my "essence" at home. I was operating on completely outdated leadership principles that no longer work believing that I needed to be someone else to be able to do my job, lead a group of staff and be successful. I was equating "living and working from the heart" to weakness!

And then my coach introduced me to an entirely foreign idea. 'What if I was to honor my staff's tears.' What if ... ? That was a lot to take in all at once.

The conversation left me beaten, exhausted, deflated but extremely grateful. What followed was a heartbreaking and incredibly rewarding process of coming to a realization that I need to really take a long look at "who I am and how I show up in the world" versus "how I want to show up".

Looking back and writing this story stirred up a lot of emotions! Regrets and what ifs keep coming up. But considering what happened, I am grateful that this happened. Conversations and coaching with my incredibly insightful coach led me to where I am today.

When I started looking at who I am, and how I was showing up in the world, I realized that I had been associating success with being strong, completely immersed in left brain, no room for emotions for they were a sign of weakness, and showing up with an attitude of "get it done and get it done now". However, another rude awakening was realizing that in my core that is not who I am. Here I am: full of love, carrying my feelings on my sleeve, easily excited, an eternal optimist, ready to laugh at the drop of a hat, play and celebrate, always believing nothing is impossible and communicating with the angels and dolphins. But once morning comes around, I was putting on the "suit" of a persona which felt 3 sizes too small, constricted and unattainable. I was wearing it day in and day out thinking that is how I make a difference and that is the way to lead. Oh no! That is not how I wanted to live my life.

Realizing what is going on is one thing. Actually stepping into it and making change is another. It takes intentional awareness and mindfulness. I knew this was going to be a bit of a challenge considering how long I have been carrying the habits and the beliefs that were no longer working, nor serving me. So, I started to experiment. It can be hard to "shed" old habits all at once. So, I started to take a little piece of real me to work every day. Once I felt comfortable with that, I went on to experiment with taking another part of real me to work while shedding the part that did not even belong to me to begin with. Bit by bit, real me woke up and real me went to work. The truth is, I am an intuitive who communicates with the angels and the dolphins. I am also the leader of a nonprofit organization; a role I carry for forty or more hours a week.

First I was whispering that I am an intuitive, angel and dolphin communicating, nonprofit executive director! And then I was able to say it out loud! The more I said it the more it became me!

I've come a long way since then. Today, my heart leads the way in all my leadership decisions. I have come to understand that leadership is not "leading" people to something or "leading" them to do something I want. It is being an example, leading the way to remove any and all road blocks so that others can rise and shine as leaders in their own right. It is creating a sacred space where they can be who they are without fear of repercussions, and shed tears or laugh their hearts out if they want to! It is empowering others, affirming and validating them. It is building on their gifts and talents. It is about being willing to be led and taught. It is about willing to be vulnerable. It is about responding, not reacting; it is about asking, "how can I lovingly handle this situation" in the best interest of everyone involved.

I am learning to let my right brain bring out the best of my left brain. I still have to make hard decisions at times that may not be the first choice of everyone involved. I still have to tap into that logical left brain of mine to make certain business decisions. However, the days of leading from someone else's point of view are long gone.

I am perfectly aware of the fact that I am a "misfit" among my female nonprofit leader peers. I am absolutely okay with that because the peace I gained during this process is worth every single "raised eyebrow." And being the eternal optimist that I am, I trust that more of us will be leading through both the heart and the mind for neither of them are exclusive of each other. I keep *stepping in* more and more to who I truly am wherever I am! It feels so good, so freeing and so delicious that I can taste it everyday!

Oh, and the staff person whose tears were the catalyst to my awakening to a leadership that makes my heart soar? She did cry one more time about a few months after all this started. I told her, I honor her and her tears and reaffirmed how much I trust her, her gifts and her talents and that I have absolute faith she will be successful in carrying out the responsibilities of her position. That was 3 ½ years ago. She is still with us, creating change, making things happen successfully. Now days, we all cry time and again… but it is all tears of joy and happiness or because we have been deeply touched by something in our core.

All is well and journey goes on!

Nukhet Govdeli Hendricks, is a gifted intuitive who channels the divine guidance of the angels and the dolphins for those who are seeking to gain clarity to live their most spirited and sparkling lives. It is Nukhet's soul mission to be a bridge to the angelic realm; to assist others on their path to divine love and light, and to connect them to their innermost wisdom, that divine spot within. Nukhet, a native of Turkey who moved to the USA in 1987, lives in West Fargo, ND with the love of her life husband Bryan, daughter Abby, and her cats Hobo and Kiki. Visit Nukhet's website at www.nukhets.com.

Story Four

Kindness and Support is a Strength

Natalie Forest

It seems I am still learning the same lesson. A big event for work is one week away and it will likely be a more chaotic event than in previous years. This time I jumped in and helped a colleague who had been complaining for weeks that it is too much work and he can't do it all. I helped him, spending hours of my time only to be told "this is unacceptable" and "you have no clue" so do not dare to touch this part of the event. I was stunned. Well, honestly, looking back, I was more amazed and bewildered. This is a male; an older male, quite entrenched in his ways and here I am a much younger, successful, and capable woman. It was a storm waiting to happen. Looking at the last 2 days, I guess I knew it had to come to this and that is why I am so calm. Calm and standing my ground.

It is sad that in the 21st century in an era that is supposed to be open-minded, collaborative and service-oriented the old prevails. Though many people in higher positions are on my side they are not taking action because this male has longevity and because there are so many other things that are more pressing right now. What is more pressing than enabling the smooth flow of an event that acknowledges the hard work of young people?

All of this is in the back of my mind while I'm taking a few minutes to decompress. I hear my daughter waking up. My husband speedily gets up to try and get her back to sleep since he knows I need a few minutes of downtime. But, my daughter won't be calmed down. I hear her voice "I want mommy." I feel myself getting weak as I hear her voice over the monitor. Weak in the sense of motherly love. Weak in the sense of "I need to be there for her, strong for her." Weak in the sense of putting myself last again. Service. Service. Service.

When I was a young girl in Germany, it seemed that everyone looked at me as leading, as being able to lead regardless of how old I was. I remember the questions put in front of me. The answers I gave almost sounded like someone else was providing them. I was detached. I wanted to be detached because knowing what I knew and fully understanding that I knew with 99% accuracy could be scary. At that age, I just gave the answers with confidence. Then I grew up, grew older and tried to phrase the answer with the same honesty and with a little bit of sugar-coating. I began to veil things a little, the way we do when we do not wish to cause harm. I knew that what I cared most about were living beings and trying to make their lives the best possible, the happiest possible. Even then I knew that if I could not facilitate that it was time for me to leave to go somewhere else and help there.

So now, all grown up, in my second marriage, with a child I look back. I hear my daughter. I see my husband. I look around at all those who look to me for help and I know. I have to be strong. It's that motherly strength. My husband put it something like this, "it's like that analytical mindset that is needed but always focused on 'what do people need' and then you go and make it happen." Like parents. We may not always have the experience and still we know what is needed. We'll do things for our children because we care so much. When focus is required I get really calm. It's like directing an orchestra, seeing all the different pieces, intuitively knowing how they fit and allowing them to have a voice while joining into a most beautiful choir.

That choir is part of my nature. I see the vision of what is possible every day of my life. I push the limits to get there - so that we all can be ourselves, be authentic and amazed at who we are. Yet, how do I get us there? There are days when I am tired and only those close to me see that. There are days when I go into my office in our house and I just sit down. There are days when all I want is a hug, not a position of leadership.

I remember walking into a new job about 9 or 10 years ago and after the first couple of days of getting organized and meeting people one co-worker came up to me. This older, kind gentleman stood in front of me. He looked at me. Then he said, "So, when are you going to be President here?" I remember not knowing what to say at first. Then I said, "I don't want to be that. I just want to be here and do the best I can to help." Ten years later this conversation is still with me as this kind of attitude from others has been a constant companion. However quietly I walk into a room, however much I try to blend in – people look at me as if I am the one they have been waiting for in that room. I often find myself saying, "Oh no, I'm just here to learn" for which I get bewildered looks and heads shaking.

I've been trying to hide for so long, not from myself, not from my duties but from the category "leader." Hiding from that old masculine image of a leader. I saw that in action this past Friday. A small woman was leading a meeting. She made her opinions clear, raised her voice, interrupted others and prevented some discussions and some voting by her actions. Bully – is what I thought and I saw that her leadership style was the "old masculine" and it made my heart hurt. I felt myself shut down from listening to her and just observing the energies. The funny thing is that when I walked in many people who were present thought I was there to take charge. Once again, I had to explain that I was not. Leading a supposedly collaborative meeting that way had me shiver, literally.

When I lead it's all about listening, hearing, taking in and allowing all to be heard. Many powerful women are conditioned to remain behind the limelight. We forget our power. We forget how we lead. Kindness and compassion – two of the most powerful forces in the world and they can overthrow the way the world works, which is why they are so fear- invoking.

There was a day when I realized my marriage was over and it was time for me to take the lead in ending it. Until then it had been like a challenge to see how long I could suffer, how long I could try to save him and forfeit me. I had a conversation with a dear friend who said, "How long can you take this? " and I took that as a challenge; "Don't dare me" to prove that I could save my now ex, that I could survive putting everything and everyone before me. Then, I woke up. My body was screaming out. I was sick a lot. And then there was that fight. Screaming, yelling – you can see that in movies. Until, suddenly I was watching us argue. I was almost floating above the situation realizing how silly this yelling was, how non-sensical the accusations were because no one was right, we were dealing with emotions and they are never wrong just maybe not in agreement. So while I was there, observing from atop, I became quiet and calm. The whole situation changed. The scene changed. My husband stopped talking. He just looked at me. I saw sadness come over him and we both knew. It was done. We knew but I still had to take the lead and finish it. I had to take the lead in being grateful for all that happened during the marriage and really "divorcing" from that. This was my way to re-learn detachment in that positive way that I was able to do as a child.

That detachment was crucial. That gratitude took a lot of time and work but I had cats and family still depending on me. More than that, I had me depending on me. This is where I took a leap of faith back to me. I needed to re-find me. Anyone standing in the way needed to be shut out for a while. I remember how difficult it was not to answer the phone when mom rang. Or not to run to a friend who needed me. I remember that because this was something I had not done before: putting me first. If I did not put me first, I could not serve those that needed me the most. I did not argue about this. I did not protest about it. I just did it. I know it hurt some people when I took my time and my space. For the best of all, that higher purpose, I had to. I could no longer deny myself healing if I was to continue really helping others.

Looking back I've always had both sides, masculine and feminine. My leadership was usually quiet with no title. I didn't need the official position. I am the "911 facilitator" as I was called just this Thursday – always there to rescue a situation, a discussion, an event when it seems to fail. I am driven by purpose. Yes, the higher purpose. Yes, the quiet leader. Yes, the facilitator. Yes, the supporter who connects people and helps them shine. That's what I do. That's what I love.

I enjoy the background and try and avoid the limelight. I meet and work with those who push me towards that light, who help me grow into that arena where everyone's watching. Funny how the limelight seems to seek me... It requires me to step out into that light to teach, to facilitate, to support and empower others to BE. It's the ancient hero story, I suppose. The leader who would prefer to be home, bake cookies and prepare dinner in return for a warm, long hug and a kiss.

Many successful female leaders share patterns of embracing wisdom and conversation. Leaders, such as Indira Gandhi, Mother Theresa have shared more of that feminine side, understanding that even the female needs to "put her foot down" from time to time. I have learned from them and there are many women leaders like me who are working through kindness and love and will not let their values be trampled upon. We do draw a line and anyone who crosses it will be called up on it, with assertive motherly love.

So here we are and I will share what I think good leadership is:

1. Living by example
2. Living by truth, honesty, and integrity
3. Understanding and knowing yourself

4. Vulnerability and admission of weaknesses and strength
5. Ability to listen, learn, and share
6. Being an inspiration to others
7. Being part of a team
8. Being significant

I work on that every day. Every night I reflect on where I am and how I can do better. Every day I aim to help make peoples' lives happier and if I cannot. I will move on to the next place. I will leave in a heartbeat if my service is no longer needed or when I am not contributing to improvement – that scares a lot of people, too. Ha, I left a very powerful job after having created something magnificent because the values of the overseeing office did not align with mine. My values cannot be comprised because I live by example. I admit my shortcomings.

As Albert Einstein said, "Most of the things that are really worth knowing cannot be taught, they must be learned" and we usually learn within the environment in which we are raised. I was raised by a single mother; I lived in a society that was focused on society moving forward and helping those less fortunate; even though there was some competition in the end everyone was – to some degree – supportive due to the knowledge that if the society did not work together, the society would fall apart. That is a very important lesson in history and humanity.

As I am putting the finishing lines on this writing it is time again for me to detach, to leave some things behind so that I can serve more and better. It is never quick or easy but it becomes easier every time. When the signs are clear that is time to leave, I must. I am here to serve, lead and teach. I have learned this lesson well.

Natalie Forest is a mom, student of life, and loves to bake! With a Ph.D. in History, years of teaching about the consistencies in history, the reasons behind "what happened" and helping learners explore alternatives, Natalie Forest is taking her expertise in history, coupled with her long-standing mentoring to females and female entrepreneurs across the globe. As a speaker, executive coach, and mentor Natalie helps you revolutionize YOUR potential by liberating your life so you can BE all you are. Natalie, the teacher, walks with you as you learn to interrupt negative patterns and create new ones that get you to your dream.
https://www.life-transforming.com/

Story Five

Some Day is Now

Sandy McDougall

"Some day I am going to stand up in front of people and speak from my heart."

I was a six-year old standing in the middle of a large family gathering, everyone else oblivious to my silent, life-changing revelation. What was a little girl in the early 1960's to do with such a knowing and big vision for her future?

When my family or extended family gathered for meals or for our frequent celebrations, someone always spoke from the heart. By the age of six, I had heard countless speeches, poems, songs, blessings, and welcoming comments in the context of these gatherings. From a very young age, we children knew what the chiming sound of knife on crystal glass meant: time to fall silent and listen.

In our family tradition however, that kind of speaking was reserved for the men. Somehow, it never occurred to my little girl self to expect anything different. I was also aware that the men in our family stood up to speak in places beyond our homes. Many were local, regional, and national leaders, and it had been so for several generations.

While I grew up in the presence of leaders and speakers and probably absorbed a lot from being around such modeling, I was a grown woman with children before I saw any woman in my family stand up to speak. And they were members of the next generation after mine. In my childhood, many of the adult women in my family held themselves proudly, but they stood either beside or behind their men. They might be well spoken, but they sat in the front row while their men spoke at the podiums. The unspoken message was that women could not or should not take that place up front.

So it was not surprising that my young mind could not possibly imagine living the truth of my six-year old revelation. I must have tucked my "some day " memory far back into my subconscious mind because I completely forgot that confident childhood moment of knowing for decades.

Interestingly enough, for someone who witnessed many speakers and knew she wanted to speak, I was an extremely quiet and reserved little girl. I preferred things I could "do" without saying very much. Perhaps I knew that I had to widen my life experience to discover my own unique voice. I left home at sixteen, yearning to discover more about life and about myself.

I lived abroad for a year after high school, experiencing new cultures and norms. Then, as fate would have it, I attended a university in the mid 70's in a time of much social change. I witnessed students from all backgrounds actively and publicly advocating for themselves and for others, for choice, and for new ways to communicate and work together.

Although I was intrigued with what I saw, I was not quite ready to speak up about these things myself. I felt like a babe in the woods. I had begun to read extensively about the challenges facing women, past and current. Volunteer work in a women's shelter gave me first hand experience of some of the worst that can happen to women who are not able to speak up for themselves. My awareness was growing.

Then, in my mid twenties, I saw a listing in my local newspaper:

"New cooperative household seeks members. Call to set up interview."

Something in me felt an irresistible magnetic attraction to those ten simple words, compelling me to call and inquire.

Within weeks, I packed my belongings and became a member of a fledgling cooperative community of seven young adults. Together, we co-created a vibrant living environment that lasted seven years. Through those experiences, I learned a whole new way to think, see, feel, act, and live. And I began to find my own voice.

We were mainly young adults interested in trying something new. Then there was Elaine. Though she only lived with us a few short months, Elaine brought tangible skills and experience in intentional collaborative process and she stayed long enough to pass them on to us. She had been a member of a national network of social activist collectives dedicated to social change through peaceful action. She taught us the fundamentals of collaborative process and consensus decision-making, and these tools helped us create a close-knit, well run, and mutually respectful community.

Together, we built an ongoing process which encouraged each of us to speak up, as well as to respect each other's opinions and needs. I was experiencing first hand the potential of conscious process for empowering each individual as well as strengthening the group.

After growing up in a culture where certain voices dominated, and where decision-making was centralized, I had stumbled on an inclusive communication process where every voice counted for something. It felt refreshing, freeing, and so right. Transparent inclusive process became my preferred modus operandi.

Despite my new tools, something invisible still held a tight grip on me and kept me from standing up to speak from my heart. Of course, I was no longer a little girl. I was in fact a financially independent, well-educated young professional woman with plenty of leadership potential living hundreds of miles away from my family of origin. Still, looking back, I can see how my sub-conscious mind continued to believe it was inappropriate and maybe even unsafe to speak up and stand out in any way. It was as if I was scared that I would be subjected to judgment and ridicule beyond my ability to cope. I felt an irrational fear of being ostracized from my family in ways I could not bear to imagine. Something inside me desperately needed their approval. So I kept an invisible line in the sand and I would not step over it.

I had developed strong competencies in facilitating and mediating. They did not require me to stand up and voice my own thoughts, but they did give me a means to move into recognized volunteer and professional leadership roles. Although I was learning to mobilize and inspire people, I was equally careful to do so in quietly understated ways. I could and did encourage others to speak on their own behalf. I just could not do that myself.

Then an unexpected event shifted some of the blocks inside me, and ironically it happened within my family context. I was almost thirty when one of my grandmothers died. For various reasons, I was the only family member who visited that day, and it had already been several hours since she passed. I had no idea what I wanted but I followed a compelling urge.

A nurse accompanied me into the room where my grandmother's body lay. She then left us alone and closed the door. Time seemed to stop. I followed my heart. I held Gran's hand and kissed her brow. I sang our favorite hymns and songs. I told her my favorite memories of her, alternately smiling and crying at the poignant stories that came to mind. In words I had never spoken out loud, I expressed my deep love for her and an abiding appreciation for who she was and what she stood for as devoted matriarch of our family. I shed tears for the wonder of life, tears for the pain of letting go, and tears for beautiful love. I also felt the healing power of speaking from my heart.

In those moments, I became deeply aware of the great turning of the wheel of life. It was as if my grandmother was asking me to take up my part in tending and nurturing the best of our strong family spirit. Our matriarch had passed and I accepted my growing responsibility in the cycle of the generations. Before I flew back to my life far away, I insisted that I be able to speak at my grandmother's funeral. As far as I know, I was the first woman ever to stand up in front of my family - and a great many other people as well - and speak from my heart.

Now, thirty years later, I have raised my own family. My own mother is aging. I tend many of her needs since my father passed. I have also stepped forward to organize regular family gatherings to help keep our increasingly mobile family connected. I speak and act much more freely within the family arena. The events around my grandmother's death, although she herself never stood up to speak, helped me to step up, speak up, and act more confidently, visibly, and independently within my family.

Major shifts in my professional life have come more recently. A few years ago, I began to notice the arrival of what I affectionately termed "my pesky voices". They taunted me in the dark of the night. "Why are you still playing so small? You are meant to be more and do more".

What could that mean? I searched and searched my heart. Over time, I came to know that my current life mission was to inspire women to find their own voices and empower themselves more fully. That had been and still was my journey. Suddenly, time felt of the essence.

Last year, determined to step up in a big way, I presented at a local women's conference. It was the first public expression of my mission. I had facilitated countless meetings in my life. I had said a few words at my grandmother's well-attended funeral. I was just starting to write in publications. But I still had never stood up and given a full speech from my heart. I decided it was time– and I would do it at that conference.

It was a thrill to write my first speech and an even bigger thrill to give it. The whole thing felt very momentous. Little did I know at the time how truly momentous it would become for me. Just moments after my speech was over, that long forgotten memory of me at six returned to my conscious awareness, when I first knew that some day I would stand up and speak from my heart. What I had known about myself at six had taken more than fifty years to fully realize. It still takes my breath away to think of it.

I now speak, write, teach, and coach regularly on the topic of personal empowerment and living and speaking from the heart. I work with women who want to find and use their fullest, clearest voice in their lives. My work brings me unprecedented joy and fulfillment.

This past summer, I took my work on a five-week road trip, traveling solo, and connecting with many people along the way. It was hard work, risk, and playful adventure all rolled into one. Would people respond to my message and maverick energy, and be inspired to seek out their own powerful and authentic voice and mission? They did. I was once again breaking the spell of convention in my life.

Over the years, as I learn to live life on my own terms, I see how some things have held me back and others have become a source of strength. My life journey was anything but linear. I followed my heart one choice and one step at a time. It was a leaning in. Nobody gave me my voice. I had to learn how to use it. Nobody gave me my power. I had to learn how to take it. And all the while, it helped to keep my ears, eyes, and arms open - and my heart willing.

And finally, more than fifty years later, my some day has become my now.

Sandy McDougall spent decades being a hard-working, responsible woman. She completed 2 degrees, raised 3 sons, learned 4 languages, lived in 5 states, served on 6 boards of directors, competed in 7 different sports, and held 8 different jobs. Recently, she reclaimed her fun-loving Maverick spirit. She is now an avid speaker, writer, inspirational coach, and advocate for successful Maverick working and living. Sandy is the creator of the Maverick Road Trip concept. She is also your "go-to person" if you decide that you are ready to break some mold and discover what you truly want to do and who you truly want to be. You can reach Sandy: sandy@themaverickedge.com , www.themaverickedge.com (for blogs and more) and on Facebook: https://facebook.com/themaverickedge

Part Two

I AM Transformed

"I take pleasure in my transformation. I look quiet and consistent, but few know how many women there are in me."

~Anaïs Nin

Story Six

The Year My Smallest Self Died

Sofia Wren

I sing of fear and sorrow, joy and love

The winter of 2012 I sat before my altar and contemplated. I was confused. Where was I going? I didn't know. I hoped something good lay in store for me, but I had no idea what that looked like or what I needed to do to get it.

Being someone who always has a goal, this scared me. And since so far all of my hard earned goals had failed to make me happy, I feared maybe it was hopeless. But even then I had hope to grip onto, deep down. I had also grown used to the grip of nerves. Still, I hated that pinching ache of something missing in my life.

I lit a candle and asked silently for guidance.

My hands found their way to a book, Mary Greer's *Tarot for Your Self*. I followed the instructions to use the year and my birthday to calculate a single number: 13. Flipping to the back of the book, I read that the card that described my year ahead was Death.

What does that mean? I wondered.

Maybe if I had pulled the card, I would have tried to forget. It's an eerie card, but it's hard to argue with math. It held significance to me, and uncertain though it was, it made me feel a little steadier. Curious, and still hopeful. I knew I wasn't in physical danger. Instead I wondered what would change in that year ahead? How would I change? How would my life change? I had no clue.

The pressure to figure all this out weighed heavy on me. I had to know what I was doing and fast. If I didn't know what I was doing with my life how would anyone, myself included, know that I was on track? I desperately wanted to achieve success. My whole life I'd been trying to collect triumphs to show other people. By 25 I had already changed career course three times. The lack of answers left me as I was, searching for a meaningful purpose, a way to express myself. Who am I really?

Drawn to a dream of changing the world as a diplomat, I graduated *magna cum laude* from Bryn Mawr college with a bachelor's in Political Science and a thesis in constitutional law. I loved leading in student government but by the end I knew I was too sensitive for that field in the real world. I realized this during senior year, and the rawness of my wounds living life in a harsh world drew me to counseling. It helped me some, and I thought I could do better even.

Americorps would give me experience to apply for a social work degree (career 2). But my year serving in the intercity was too draining and I was unhappy. I listened when a friend said, becoming a counselor didn't sound like me. Or did it?

My family is self-employed so I figured that was the

only way to go. I loved helping people One to One, and the signs led me to complete a Certification in Massage Therapy at 24 (career 3). I worked hard to master it but still it wasn't enough.

I wanted something deeper: to help people improve their lives dramatically, inside and out. So I asked myself over and over, "What was I supposed to do now? Where should I turn? And why did I keep choosing dead ends? Would I ever find something that felt right? Why was this so hard? What was wrong with me?"

I asked for a way forward; a sign, a message, so that I would know that I was not alone; that there was hope; that I wasn't made sensitive for nothing. I ached for significance, and yearned to serve in a bigger way, but how?

In 2012 I sat on my floor and pulled cards often. Again and again the Death card came to visit me. But knowing something needed to change didn't solve my riddle.

Having nothing else to guide me I grew into a woman who uses signs and symbols to light her way. There was no mistake that the card keep appearing.

I embraced the presence of ravens, crows and blackbirds visiting me everywhere. After I heard the birds cawing at me I googled their totem meaning. These dark-colored birds are shapeshifters, associated with death and transformation. They are connected to Goddess Morrighan of Ireland, goddess of sovereignty, magic, witchcraft, power and more.

I had asked the goddess to help my family and protect their property in 2010. I would do anything for the people I love, including ask the most powerful goddesses I can find. I can never stop loving her. She is my doorway to God and beyond. I've never spoken openly about this before, but to keep my family safe I asked for help in a ceremony that changed my life in many ways. I really opened my heart to hope and focused on a number of dreams that I had never allowed myself to imagine before.

As so many of my ceremonies do: they are beautiful to me and through them I meet a life of hopes and dreams. They give me a circle of space to breath. And every time I sit near my altar, life gets a little better. During the ceremony on the Winter Solstice 2011, just before the Year of my death, She began weaving a wider trail through my life. Guiding me towards a different way of living.

I love fiercely, and perhaps I can call myself a spiritual warrior, since I love freedom and hold shining ideals. But without Her I couldn't bear the trials of everyday life, working at jobs that did not use all of me. It is her I have to thank for my life now, as I move closer to the fullest and truest expression of what I hold dear.

Only recently have I begun to spin my truth out in the open, but even when I thought I had no option but to hide, living a day without Her was unbearable--this powerlessness, those feelings of loss and sadness, old family wounds coming up to ache anew, loneliness, different, strange, misunderstood, misfit feelings. Even if they weren't something that many people experience, the burden was too heavy for me to breath. The touch of the divine feminine lightened my load, like air under feathers.

Seeing the birds flying in the sky, resting on a light post, or landing in front of my car so suddenly that I had to break to a stop, quickly became comforting to me, rather than scary. They encouraged me, and cheered me on.

Maybe I did matter, enough for the Universe to care. Even though I was nobody since I was on track to nowhere the birds kept coming my way. My struggle had to matter, otherwise why would the universe send me any sign at all?

The death card, the birds, told me that change was necessary and essential to stepping into my real purpose. My whole life was shifting, crumbling, breaking down and rearranging. It felt like stumbling in the dark, hoping I wouldn't fall.

My relationship to change began to shift as I realized it has always been the one constant in my life. It was nice to be able to depend on *something*. Death is a process of loss, of letting go. It's a natural part of life even if it's uncomfortable.

I had so much loss to heal. The odd one out ever since I was born bilingual, and spent my life relearning half of what I knew. My Italian mother passing at three. The ripple of sadness through my heart and the people I loved around me. The feeling of friends betraying me. Step mom.

Although I fought time I did not fight change. Soon it felt good to shed the old. I quit all four of my jobs, got more, and followed my heart to self-employment. I moved, again. I opened my heart as a daily practice.

In 2011, I was two people. During the day I had worked to pay the bills diligently with everything I had but the job didn't pay enough to be independent and didn't satisfy my soul. And in the cracks of the day, I crammed in my creativity, a courageously truthful writer protected by a pen name. Putting pen to paper was my place of worship and prayer.

As I continued into the dark chaos of the unknown, I was not alone. Gradually, the dark birds were joined by eagles. More and more soared in the sky as the weather warmed. They glide between the earth and sun, balanced, grounded and connected to Source. I aimed to be like the eagles, to let go and glide, and to trust the invisible force leading me on.

The year I pulled Death my small self died. The part of me that was hiding the Sofia that no one else had ever seen, hiding the real me. The part that didn't know what made me happy because it had shoved my natural passions so far down I had lost touch with really important things: like enjoying my off time with Epsom salt baths, petting my cat, being present with my loves, dancing, singing, painting, writing, meditation and walks in nature.

Death killed the face I hid behind, so I could find wholeness as a single person.

And singing. It was hard to sing into the microphone at the beginning of 2013. Years before I had sang at a talent show in front of 250 peers, but I couldn't sing lyrics to one of my favorite songs from high school to ten people in a basement. My voice choked and I forgot the words. And it stung, knowing I could do better.

Taking voice lessons was the best thing I ever did. Spring of 2013.

I leapt into full time self-employment even as my private massage practice transformed into something else entirely. I quit my day job, and questioned my sexuality. I turned on my video camera, wrote and shared. I had private sessions with amazing women for practicing my intuitive skills.

I wasn't sure if I was ready to let anyone see me, because I didn't have it all figured out but I did it anyway, and that's how I found Sofia Wren.

Sofia Wren is a unique bird with many talents.

She sings. She dances. She heals. Her words and voice linger. She shares, inspires, and educates. Sweet in silence. Spot on. Playful but old deep down with sass. She is a quiet friend and an outgoing speaker. Opening to love her makes everything else in the world flow easily.

Since 2013, working with a tribe of sensitive and passionate women with businesses as Sofia Wren, I have learned that whenever any of us reach forward to fly bigger and chase more challenging dreams--the ones that we truly want, that we would rather squelch than ruin by failing--that's when the scary stuff happens. That's when we get overwhelmed and uncertain, and when our adrenaline is pumping day and night.

When it comes down to it there are only two roads.

One is full of challenges, and responsibilities: should do this or that to deserve or not, to fail or succeed, to be good enough. Have to play the game to get over the mind and muscle bending hurdles. This obstacle course is the road my small self thought was the safe path. It was a way to run from what I might lose, but I had to reach a successful destination to arrive at happily ever after one day. But on this path the mind games never end, never slow, and that hoped for happily ever after never arrives. That success is clearly visible over the hill but more obstacles appear as soon as last is conquered.

The other road is lighter, so bright and hazy that the end is unclear though you have a loose idea of where it goes. It feels amazing to take the scenic route, which is comfortable, fun, open and easy. There is no knowing what to expect around the corner. The only guidance comes from the heart pulling you forward one step at a time.

We can battle and fight for success, or we can surrender our fixed long term plan and take it one joyful day at a time.

For so long, I feared sharing my unique perspective would scare everyone away, but once I truly allowed myself true expression, I learned how wrong I was. Instead I drew people closer. Sharing truth- messy as it is, is the only way to reach other people who understand and exude compassion, admiration and love.

My lesson was to trust that fear of the death, the darkness, the shedding and mess of the old falling away around the new is all a part of the process of birthing something amazing. Fear of time passing me by without leaving a mark on this world-- as I am all that is left of my mother dying so young--is the only reason I am motivated to use my time to the fullest, and I have come to be thankful for that encouragement!

I let people in to see the journey. Each time I dared to share my life as it unfolded in raw form, I found support. I found other women reflecting back, turning the mirror of their gaze around to show me their view of me: a flame shining in the darkness, spreading love through truth to others all around me.

I wanted to help people to heal in the deepest way possible, and not just the physical.

Because I knew then that the lines between mind body spirit are arbitrary, just like the lines between masculinity and femininity, strength and weakness. I wanted to weave it all together and heal the divides that kept our pains separated and locked away from everyone else, and even our self. My sharing didn't just help me, it gave others inspiration, too.

Death killed the numbness that hid the truth from me-- that by hiding I stood in my own way. I knew it was time to break the silence and start some conversations and to do that, I had to allow my voice to be heard. I learned that vulnerability and truth is a sword, the only tool that can truly vanquish the loneliness. So many of us feel so alone, despite advances in modern communication.

To allow the path to unfold unplanned is one thing, to share as a seeker is another. It is in the unknowing that truly beautiful things form, including not knowing how someone will respond after I speak about my real thoughts and feelings. Sharing that truth is how we find people who accept us for who are and not what. Letting people see us in progress is scary and so is sharing our light.

In 2012 I began writing something different than I had ever written before. My life was the inspiration. It allowed me to edit my memories, to begin to see the good in the line of mistakes that made me cringe. Still..

I decided that the only way to live in my ideal world is to write it and voice it into being.

There will always be people who will put my book aside, decide I'm not their cup of tea. But in my ideal world, I have every right to be here, and to say what I think. It's the only way forward and it's become my mission to help other sensitive good-hearted people get back in touch with their voice, intuition and power to break through the confusion so we can create a beautiful world together.

From childhood, nature has always been my solace. Death and reality were too harsh at times, as the universe pulled loved ones into oblivion. I lived between the worlds, the dreamer in the backseat, watching the world on the other side of the window, and looking for the hope.

I used to wish I were somewhere else-- a fantasy land. I thought I didn't have the power to go to another place. I still hoped.

But now I am on a different map entirely, enjoying the ride to nowhere. And fantasies cannot compare to living for the beauty in the moment.

This is my life. This is my world. Hear my song. Now sing yours.

Sofia Wren shows sensitive women who dream of helping people with their gifts, including through a business or creativity come out of hiding. She teaches how to have more confidence and be more creative so women can easily achieve their goals and bust through their limitations. Teaching them how to speak up about what they really think and feel. Using Intuition. Learning Trust. Increasing Money and Fun. She lives in Baltimore, Maryland, and adores angels, goddesses, cats, the ocean, crystals, roses, singing, salt baths, writing, and heart to heart connections. She is a Certified Ethical Intuitive Consultant, Coach, angel columnist and mind-body-spirit healer. She offers free strategy sessions by application at www.sofiawren.com

Story Seven

Leading the Next Generation

Kristen Rockenbach

As I started writing, my story was going to be about my career in male dominated fields, Physics and IT Consulting. I was always able to get promoted quickly and be very successful using the typical male leadership traits. I had completed more than half my story, when my life took a crazy turn and made me reexamine what feminine leadership was in my life.

At this time in my life, I was happily married to my husband, Joe. We had created our ideal life, a nice home just big enough for us, our two dogs, Baxter and Manola, and to be able to have friends and family over. We decided early in our relationship that we would not have children. We loved each other and were very content with our life full of family, friends, travel, and spontaneity.

It all started with a phone call from my sister, telling Joe and me that our nephew was going to be in summer school because he failed history. At the time, we asked how we could help support him not only with summer school but also in the fall. How could we work with him to help him get into college? Summer school went by quickly and he did well. We thought he was back on track until the fall, when five weeks into school we found out that he was failing EVERY class. We all knew that we had to take drastic action, but what? I volunteered to help get him into boarding school and become his legal guardian. Legal guardian. I didn't ask to become anyone's legal guardian. It wasn't part of my life plan. I didn't want to take on the role of "mother" or "caregiver." I was angry. I had a wonderful life and this would mean big changes that I didn't want. The little voice in my head whispered back, "If not you, then who?" I knew I had to step into this new role.

I was consumed for a week researching schools, and then talking to admissions officers. What would be a good fit for him? I knew nothing about high school, let alone boarding school. I settled on three very different schools: a progressive school in the Berkshire mountains that doesn't even give grades, an all boys traditional boarding school in the foothills of the Blue Ridge mountains, and a military school outside of DC. He could choose any school he was accepted to.

I planned to go to New York to break the news to him and help complete all three applications over one weekend. My mother, sister, nephew and I went to dinner. It was great, the four of us together. It had been a very long time since we were all together, just the four of us. Then came time to let him know his life was going to change drastically. I was the only woman around the table with no parental experience but I was the one who broke the news. My heart ached, my stomach was in knots, and I could hardly breathe. We love him so much but this is hurting him. I watched helplessly as he cried at the table. He thought we were sending him away; we didn't love him; he was stupid. That is not the truth! We love him more than anything. The pain would subside but the waiting and watching was excruciating. BREATHE just BREATHE, I kept telling myself. He needed to move through the pain in his own time. As can be imagined, there was initially a lot of anger and refusal, and within a few hours acceptance had begun to settle in.

The next day I worked with him to complete the applications. I guided him through many questions of self-discovery and introspection. While lighting the path from behind, I had to allow him to lead the way.

After an exhausting 24 hours of breaking the news and completing applications, I went to bed. I was sleep deprived, like a new mother. Questions swirled in my head. Will it be ok? What else can I do? Is this the right thing? Sleep did not come quickly, only planning, worrying, and hoping. Everything was changing. My life would never be the same. What would my life look like now? How do you welcome a 16 year old into your home, but not be his mother?

Joe and I needed to set expectations not rules. We needed to give him a room. We were starting to create a patchwork family. Our "alone time" schedules would be around his vacations, weekends home with us or getting him to the airport to be home with his mother. We needed to give him the structure while still giving him freedom to make his own decisions and mis-takes.

At each campus visit and interview, I was so nervous for him. I had to take a backseat, let him be the one to answer the questions. He had to stand on his own. Would he like the schools we picked out? Would he be able to see himself there? Would he be homesick? Would he fit in? Oh, what have I signed up for? Can I do this? What if I screw up?

When you say yes to have your world shaken up; miracles start to happen. After seeing all the schools, he was excited to go. He understood why the small classes with more individual attention would help him. The applications really made him look at the path he was going down and where that would lead. This was a turning point for him to say YES to a different future. In just a few days we saw him really mature. With all the school visits over and applications in, it was a waiting game. Which schools would he get into? Which school would he choose?

WAITING... WAITING... WAITING...

As we waited to hear from the schools, we had to follow-up with teachers to make sure they sent their recommendations and records. It seems like it took forever to have everything submitted for evaluation.

The night before he was to stay with us again, I had an "Oh Shit" moment of wanting what is best for him and letting go to allow him to grow. He had just found out that he was not accepted into the counselor-in-training program at the camp he went to in the summer. He had wanted to get in so badly, only 14 slots for 40 boys is tough competition. How do I comfort him, through such a disappointment? My own heart ached helplessly wanting all the good for him and his heart's desires to come true. Again the small voice in my head, "Help him see the value in the lesson of disappointment." This will happen again. What doors will now open that wouldn't have been before? What will take the space that has been cleared? Love lessons are the hardest to experience.

As I was going through all of this with him, I remembered the Passion Test that I took weeks before we learned he was failing out of school. From the test, I learned that one of my passions is to influence people to create a better world. Inheriting a 16 year old was not what I had in mind when I wrote that. It is something bigger than I thought I would ever do. Having this perspective comforts me. I know that this is in alignment with who I AM and where my path is taking me. I don't have to worry so much. The universe will provide the miracles to support us through it. And still I have doubts sometimes. Will I be able to do this? What am I modeling to him? What is he taking in from what he observes?

Finally we heard from the schools; he got into his top two choices but not the third. He was so excited to go to his top choice. Now we had to kick it into high gear because he would start right after Thanksgiving; Lots to do and buy to get him ready, not to mention paperwork and more paperwork to complete.

As I was on my way to the airport for a quick business trip, I got a call from my sister. She wouldn't sign the legal guardian papers. I was enraged. My cheeks were flushed. I was sweating. All I felt was burning hatred towards her. It was because of her that he is in this mess. NOW SHE CARES??? I just wanted to scream and cry. I had tried to have compassion and to support her but I can't now. I wanted to say that I am acting in his best interest, but AM I? Is it old family dynamics? Is it my ego? I was stepping into something I never wanted nor asked for. I believed this was the right thing to do. I was not willing to take on the responsibility if I had no authority. I was clear about that. Hopefully we could get to some sort of agreement. Suddenly, I felt unappreciated for all that Joe and I had done for my nephew and my sister.

Throughout the next few weeks, our nephew spent time with Joe and me for the visits and preparing for his new school. We even took him on a tour of a local university so he saw the goal. He understood what he needed to do now to set himself up for the future. As he spent more time with us, I realized that I needed to explain "the what" and "the why." He observed every word and action. I repeatedly asked myself questions. What do I want to show him? What example do I want to be? I had to choose my words carefully. What is he seeing and hearing? I had to be TRANSPARENT. I wanted him to see everything, to make his own decisions, to understand the thought behind the action.

With each stay, he made his room more his own. He moved furniture, he talked about what color he would paint it on his first break. We needed to get bunk beds for him and the dog. He shares the bedroom Baxter, our 128-pound Mastiff/ St Bernard mix, claimed as his own. As ridiculous as it is, Baxter sleeps in the twin bed but shares it when our nephew is with us.

As our nephew spends more time with us, he and Joe get closer. I am a little jealous of things they share. I feel like the "odd man out". I want "our" time back. I don't want to have to share Joe. How do I keep it together? I have been so engrossed in helping our nephew; I missed important things on my own calendar like a gathering of my priestess sisters, which was planned months earlier. How do parents work and still give the attention to their children and spouse? How do single parents manage?

And just like that a month and a half have gone by and we are moving him into his dorm. He is making new friends and can't get rid of us fast enough. It is done, but really it is just beginning. I have done all I can.

Epilogue:

Joe and I will continue to provide him love, support, guidance, and a home, since my sister finally signed the custody papers. He completed his first year at boarding school and is doing well. He passed his sophomore year with a B average, played on the basketball and baseball teams, learned that singing was a passion and talent that he didn't know before, and is looking forward to going back in the fall. My sister and I have joint custody and are co-parenting. She too has grown a lot through the process and become a feminine leader in her own right.

It is now up to him to make what he will with the opportunities he has been given. I reflect on: What does feminine leadership mean to me? It is the soft but strong hand that guides those around her. It is the ability to nurture while still pushing forward. It is staying rooted and grounded but swaying and bending to the elements as necessary.

This whole experience has brought me closer to everyone in my family. With my new understanding, I happily step in to the Mother phase of my life to lead the next generation.

Kristen Rockenbach lives outside of Washington DC with her husband and two dogs. She founded Tuckahoe to bring heart and soul back into corporations and to support the health and vitality of the companies and the people that make them up. Tuckahoe helps organizations and individuals realize their potential to thrive by influencing leaders to leave a legacy of joy and equality. Kristen holds an MBA in Management Information Systems and BS in Physics. She is an active member in the community, volunteering with Junior League of Washington, University Club of DC, and Pets on Wheels. Follow her on twitter @Krockenbach www.TuckahoeLLC.com

Story Eight

"the ambition of Nature"

Jacke Schroeder

"Just because you complete this program doesn't mean you will become one," she said.

"What?! "

"There's only one requirement for becoming a Prayer Intercessor in the Heavenly Court," said Rabbi Ruth.

"Well, what's the requirement?"

"You must commit that for the rest of your life you will never judge another person."

"That's impossible!"

Two weeks of training left to go and just now Rabbi Ruth is telling us this? I can't commit to that! I'll never be able to do that!

*****

Seven years later, I was preparing my first Sacred Pearl Tour to Israel. Before scheduling the pilgrimage I was in Brooklyn visiting one of my Rabbis. For some inexplicable reason I asked him if he thought I should lead the pilgrimage with a group of women or first, go myself? The last time I was in Israel was during the summer after my high school graduation. He paused, looked within, and said, "Go yourself first and then you can lead."

I didn't like his answer. I didn't want to go alone. *I shouldn't have asked,* I thought to myself.

Immediately after I left him and got into my car to drive back home, the telephone rang. It was the owner of the supporting tour company calling to let me know she had just found an airfare for my group that was so low she couldn't believe it. She said she hadn't seen prices like those for years. I sat on my inner resistance and rebellion fence for all of two minutes and said, "Yes, reserve 20 seats!"

While planning activities and choosing teachers I wanted to provide for the women pilgrims, I thought of her, Rabbi Ruth Gan Kagan. She had taught me from Jerusalem over the telephone, 5889 miles from where I was located. I knew she still was in Jerusalem. To my surprise, I didn't feel any pull to contact her, or any desire to plan any kind of meeting with her once we arrived in Israel.

Everything else fell easily into place—a private and flexible English speaking tour guide, boutique spa hotels, inexpensive airfare, a supporting U.S. based tour company to arrange all of the reservations and payments, even to the extent that every special person in Israel who I wanted to teach us answered their telephones when I called them from America. It was as if a red carpet was rolled out the minute I decided I wanted to lead a women's pilgrimage to Israel. I couldn't wait to go. Until...

No one booked!

My Rabbi tuned in to what my soul wanted, what I really wanted, what I wouldn't acknowledge to myself. I wanted to go alone, in other words, the itinerary I put together was the pilgrimage I wanted for myself!

I didn't want to go completely alone though. I wanted Jackeman, my Beshert, my soul mate, to go, too. I wanted him to have the experience of a lifetime. And, I felt concerned if I went and he didn't that a wide gulf would form between us that would be difficult to cross or close upon my return home. With some convincing, 10 days before departure he agreed to join me.

Was it synchronicity, or was it something else? Jackeman's airline ticket was ridiculously inexpensive, even less than my already great price, which I had gotten months earlier. And he hadn't seen his passport in a long while, but when he found it he discovered that it was only weeks away from expiring. His passport was at the end of its 10-year shelf life. We were both so excited!

Something I wasn't able to define had begun stirring in me. It was subtle, but I could feel it and it wasn't positive. Slowly, I noticed small judgments and occasional harsh condemnations of Jackeman creeping into my thoughts. Phew, that scared me.

As soon as we arrived in Israel, and I caught a whiff of the culture, I felt very shy of public displays of affection. No. Not just shy. Downright rudely refusing to be touched, even to just have my hand held. This was extremely unusual behavior for me. Never before did being touched by Jackeman in public bother me. When he attempted to simply touch my arm or shoulder I felt enraged!

When thinking of whether or not to go to Israel without Jackeman and the gulf that might form between us, perhaps what was really going on was forewarnings of what was ahead. It was my out-of-the-ordinary behavior with him in public that actually created that wide gulf. What was worse, in a short amount of time those feelings and behaviors extended into our private time and space. It didn't only feel as if we were strangers, it felt like we were enemies!

This continued. Some days were more bearable than others. And of course we each were engrossed in our experience of traveling to 41 places in 10 days, including the Holiest sites. We each carried a memory of why we were there and that we loved each other, and because of that we were able to share messages coming to us through the ancient rocks and walkways. We shared our intuitions and dreams, and our awe of the land, the food, and the people.

Our hearts and souls were being broken open. Intermixed with the goodness that flowed out, it felt like long-lodged "poison." I was lost in judgment and condemnation, distancing myself. And he was too. The more judging and condemning, the more it seemed as if a force was controlling us. It was a vicious flow back and forth, inside and outside, over and over again! Anger, repulsion, the darkest kind of condensed negativity that can bubble up in people from time to time was spewing from our pores. During periods of time on some days it felt nearly intolerable. I prayed and prayed to be relieved of the harshness, the clamping down, the misunderstanding of the thoughts and feelings and reactions.

Finally the lid blew off the container that was barely holding this force. Like a volcano, the frustration, disappointment, intolerance, and anger erupted out of Jackeman! It sounded like the uncorking of a champagne bottle. The soul filled earth, the ancient crust, cracked open and the toxic antediluvian negativity escaped.

At that, I had an epiphany! A Divine orchestration for a symphony intended to bring cleansing and a return to wholeness for both of us was at play. We were both being spiritually cleansed!

The next day we arrived at Magdala, ("Migdal," named after the old city of Migdala Nunia), a city by the Sea of Galilee about 7 km. north of Tiberias. Magdala was a wealthy Galilean town, destroyed by the Romans in the First Jewish-Roman War (66CE-73CE) at the time of the destruction of the Second Temple in 70CE. It is said to be the hometown of Mary Magdalene. The moment our car came to a stop at Magdala and I looked out across the ruins, my body began to rapidly vibrate. Instantly, I went on high alert!

This large-scale archeological excavation and the Magdala ruins are administered by the Catholic Church and are not generally open to the public but visible through a wrought-iron fence. It just happened that we were allowed in.

As soon as we stepped onto the site I started running around like a crazy woman. It didn't make sense at first, but I was looking for myself! I ran to the Sea, over to the salt tower, back to the fishery canals and the mikveh, back again to the Sea. I saw Jackeman watching me. I ran to him crying and told him I had lived there. He said, "And you died here!"

I have a digestive sensitivity to salt. Years prior, a psychic told me I died in a vat of salt. Migdal is an Aramaic word meaning "fish tower." The Greeks called the village Taricheia, a word meaning "pickling," because of Magdala's fish salting industry; salt towers were used for preserving and storing fish, one of the mainstays of its economy.

We were told by one of the senior archeologists that they have been able to trace Magdala as a primary city along Jesus's daily route where he would stop to preach and pray Mincha. Mincha is composed of the recitation of Psalm 145, the Amidah, a person's opportunity to approach God in private prayer and Blessings, and concludes with the Aleynu. The Aleynu is a reaffirmation of Jewish goals and a hope for the better world for all humankind. Mincha is an oasis of spiritual time in the busy workday—a moment of contemplation, a calming of nerves and a focusing of priorities.

It says in Luke 8:1-3 that Jesus began going from one city and village to another, proclaiming and preaching the kingdom of God. The twelve disciples were with Him, along with some women who had been healed of evil spirits and infirmities: Mary, called Magdalene, from whom seven demons had gone out, Joanna, the wife of Chuza, the manager of Herod's household; Susanna; and many others, who provided for them out of their means.

Yes, we were being cleansed! Magdala's location was the same general vicinity to where I lived on kibbutz when I was in Israel the first time. And throughout my life I've carried an image looking through an archway into the Golan Heights to King Herrod's castle. I knew beyond the shadow of any doubt that the life we lived in Magdala was a good life; it was a Holy life—the kind of life people aspire to live. I knew that I was one of those women who prayed with Jesus and the twelve disciples, and that I was one of those who provided for them out of our own means.

I wept with the realization that part of my soul had been left there for centuries and that it was time for me to come home to myself, to be made whole again. In order for me to be able to experience the fullness of having my soul essence returned I had to be cleansed of the "poison."

I found the place where my soul essence was wandering about; it was a rectangular shaped fenced field right next to the salt tower. I compassionately conversed with her and then gently brought her back to myself, welcoming her home into my heart.

Weeks before departing for Israel, I was speaking with my Rabbi in Baltimore, and with great enthusiasm he told me I had to spend Shabbat in Jerusalem at a very cool shul in the lower level of the Reconstructionist Synagogue. He told me it was a very unusual shul and that I would like it. Its name was Nava Tahilla, he said. He never mentioned, and I didn't ask, the name of Nava Tahilla's Rabbi. Throughout our travels, the gen of it stayed in my mind.

With jetlag and settling in when we first arrived in Israel, we didn't attend any services. It wasn't until the following Friday afternoon while driving to Jerusalem, recognizing it was close to the time for our return home, that we knew we absolutely could not go back home without having a Shabbat experience in Israel. We simply had to!

We mentioned to our tour guide that we wanted to attend Shabbat services that evening. He said he had a friend who raved about a synagogue in Jerusalem. He called her for the name and location. She answered the call, and as it turned out it was Nava Tehillah, and the Rabbi was none other than Ruth Gan Kagan!

Israel abounds in synchronicity!

When Friday night arrived, with great excitement we made our way to Nava Tehilla. Everyone sat in a circular configuration, the room brimming of young people with their children and elders. Rabbi Ruth, in the center along with the drummers and harmonium player, seemed angelic. She led and lifted everyone through devotional singing, chanting words that vibrated at the highest level of awareness. Our minds stilled, our worries dissolved, and wisdom and joy were brought forth. It felt as if we were connecting with a subtle tonic that nourished our inner being, and that imparted spiritual strength, and purified our minds and hearts.

"One may call this place the ambition of Nature, where it forces those plants that are naturally enemies to one another to agree together; it is a happy contention of the seasons, as if every one of them laid claim to this country; for it not only nourishes different sorts of autumnal fruit beyond men's expectation, but preserves them a great while; it supplies men with the principal fruits, with grapes and figs continually, during ten months of the year and the rest of the fruits as they become ripe together through the whole year; for besides the good temperature of the air, it is also watered from a most fertile fountain." —by Titus Flavius Josephus born Yosef ben Matityahu, the first-century Romano-Jewish scholar, historian and hagiographer, who initially fought against the Romans during the First Jewish-Roman War as head of Jewish forces in Galilee, speaking about the Galilee.

Things don't always resolve in neatly wrapped gifts artfully tied with pretty ribbons and bows. Just as we need to open the wrapping in order to receive and accept the gift, we must earn our gift by earnestly employing ourselves in a conscious endeavor. Like the attack by the Romans on Magdala, destroying a place amid that most fertile fountain, judgments and condemnation invade and destroy the goodness of people and relationships. Some may think bringing an end to being judgmental and condemning is something reserved for the rare few humans, such as Rabbi Ruth. I disagree. I believe this is a choice we each can make.

To reach the greatest place of love, we must choose the journey of repair and transformation. We do this by first returning to ourselves, looking within our hearts to find where it is blocked, feeling sincere regret, making confession and asking for forgiveness, and rewriting the behavioral stories of our past into new ways of thinking and acting going forward into our future. For Jackeman and I being alert to when we're judging and condemning and bringing presence and compassion to ourselves and the other, the person who is the object of such harsh treatment, is now part of our spiritual practices.

By the time we arrived in America we were back to living in our closeness. Jackeman and I acknowledge and honor our mutual love and shared spiritual journey. We remind each other of our shared value for direct communication, and making room for the other to each be both our own person and a couple. And we remain curious about the ways in which God enlightens our desires for relationship with each other and Him.

Sacred Pearl Tours "Pilgrimage to the Mother Pearl" for women of all faiths is scheduled for April 2015.

Jacke Schroeder, MSW, LCSW-C, is a shamanist, licensed counselor and energy healer, business consultant, published author, and speaker. Jacke provides personal and executive leadership development, business consulting, customized workshops, classes and speaking engagements. Jacke is the founder of Corporate Shaman U. She brings shamanism to the workplace –healing the soul of the business and its leaders— and teaches others how to bring spirit to work and tie personal growth to the bottom line. Jacke is an ordained Maggidah, an inspirational teacher and teller of stories about the journey of the soul. The founder of Sacred Pearl Tours, she leads individuals and groups on pilgrimages to sacred places. **http://sacredpearltours.com/**

Story Nine

Inside Out:
The Painful, Joy-Full Path to Feminine Leadership

Ellen Marie Dumer

"Before I formed you in the womb I knew you, And before you were born I consecrated you; I have appointed you a prophet to the nations." Jeremiah 1:5.

I never wanted this gift. When my infant self was in the "to be born" line, I didn't get a choice. The next gift in the pile was handed to me. It was "leadership" and the angel sent me down to Earth with it packed in my heart.

Looking back, the touch of God is evident. I can remember loving God even at only 4 years old. My grandmother would take me to all of her special church places. They held an "other world" mystical hold on my young soul. I could feel God there amidst the candlelight, soaring ceilings of limestone and wood trim, and the artful mosaics of the Blessed Mother. I wanted to stay there. Always. It felt like love.

In Catholic elementary school, I found the book "Bernie Becomes a Nun" in our library and took it out to read over and over again. My mom must have been thrilled because later I found out she had a nun friend who was praying for my vocation! And at one point in my life I thought I wanted to be a nun. Didn't happen, but more about that later.

While it seems an honor or a gift to pursue or envy, leadership is the most humbling gift of all. It can fool your ego into thinking you are something special and we have all seen what happens when we believe that. It knocks you far off the path from being a good leader and unless you let go of the falsely secure rope of "I'm all that" you won't be leading anything except the neighborhood strays down the alley.

My training ground was rough. But isn't everyone's? Life and its experiences is the training. The experiences that form you the most are often the most painful. They leave scars on your soul. Little merit badges on the sash you will wear to the pearly gates. You only get the badge if you really do the work. No one else can do it for you.

The gift was forced upon me at a young age, as I was caring for my younger brother and sisters and our home while my mother battled depression and cancer. Good leadership will always have a sacrificial component. Leaders are not created in a moment. Their lives create their character. Much of life twists our vision of ourselves into lies that become obstacles. These lies must be purged…it is the ironic labor pains of birth into a same, but different woman ready to stand for her passions without regard for the opinions of naysayers.

Releasing the Gift: Purging Lies and Pain from the Soul

---You can't miss the glare of the sun emanating from those patent leather shoes in this 1970 black and white photo. I see myself as a girl about 10 years old; hair in a bob, tortoise shell cat eye glasses, proudly showing off a cute sleeveless dress her mom made for her especially for this school field trip…STOP! LISTEN! FEEL! What is this?

In stealth, suddenly a heart realization intrudes and has escaped into my consciousness. Mom must have really loved me and been proud of me?! I never felt it. Or only rarely. Considering everything else going on in her life at that time, chronic illness, anxiety and depression, three other small children, she was learning to sew and taking the time to make me a dress? Am I a good girl?

What makes a good girl? Homework done with a 100% score? Chores done and checked off with no dust under the radiator for Mom's white glove test? Garden weeded and blueberries picked? Lawn mowed? Sisters and brother's lunches and dinner made? No complaining? All this and more. That's what makes a good girl…I keep trying to win the prize! Always hopeful, but always second place.

Memories come flooding back from decades ago. Where have they been stuck? My brain acting as a contortionist, deep grooves of grey matter providing a toxic sanctuary for pictures and words, thoughts and actions. An invisible door releasing emotion and memories from my brain's hiding place into my heart's anxiously pulsating vessels. My stomach seizes up, sweat brings the toxins to the surface. Fear, fear, fear. Always there... Of what?

Sending cries to wherever the soul resides, I plead to God that the spiritual residue of this time was being filtered into a more palatable vision of healing love and mercy.

I am finished.

Finished with fear.
Of the past

Casting a shadow over my now.
Wielding power over my future.

Finished with the thief.
Taking back my soul.
Snatching its pieces
One by one
Am I bleeding?

Huddled in a corner
No one see me
Please...don't look

I am not here
You don't
see...me.

It hurts.
Am I crying?

It was the day that changed everything. At 16, I was laying on my stomach in the "sunny spot" on the living room floor reading the funnies. I sensed someone else in the room. I turned my head to see my father. He had just collapsed onto the sofa. He was in his pajamas; the blue and white striped ones, the collar frayed. Black with a touch of grey hair rumpled, eyes dark and sleepless. Elbows on his knees, face in his hands. "Who was this?" I thought. And in the pit of my stomach fear made itself known with a stealthy nerve tingling whole body sensation of nausea. Fear. Again.

Then I remembered. I had answered the phone in the wee hours of the morning. He was calling from the hospital. Told me he would not be home for a while, to make sure that my sisters and brother got breakfast when they woke up and that we would not be going to church. I had barely registered the call. They happened a lot lately. Mom's in the hospital..again. Out of reach, away from us..again.

As he lifted his head out of his hands, the tears were shining over beard stubble. His voice cracked. My God, I had never seen him cry, not for anything. But his words, Your mother died last night," with those tears, showed my real father, beaten down and spent and heart-broken and scared as hell.

Expecting that.
Everyone knew.

IT was going
to happen at sometime
SOON

No big deal.
Told my sisters
and brother.
Had a viewing
Closed casket
Doesn't viewing
Mean to look at??

Didn't look when asked
BIG MISTAKE

Had a funeral
Threw some dirt
Was freezing
Bought this outfit

With you, Mom

I am NOT crying
I will NOT cry

Life rushes by without many memories when you are hiding
from grief and drowning in depression inducing self-loathing.
What came next?

Met a guy.
Fell in love.
Got pregnant
Got married
Sorry Dad
Let you down

Beautiful
baby boy

College
Study
Pregnant again
That was tough
Made it

Lovely baby girl
Happy again

Husband
Unhappy
Unhappy
Gone

Me
Wife in despair
Deep Deep despair

I am crying
I am crying
I am crying

Meet another guy.
Scared. In love.
Really? Again.
Scared silly happy real

Married
Two more daughters
…and life goes on.

And an affair begins.
The only affair allowed when you are married.

With God.

Renewed

So what happens when you fall in love with God? Your gifts become a sweet burden, one that you walk through with the confidence that you have nothing to fear; That when you put your foot in the water, its depths will not matter. Well, yes. And no.

I look back and see how God moves people and circumstances around to produce the movie of our lives. Instances when I remember God being so very present to me. All touching and important to my story. But the turning point gift was marrying the man who I met while doing a friend a favor. There are dozens of reasons why and stories of sacrifice, strife, and success. But, I know that he was put into my life to allow me to become who I am. To see who I am, in the light of his love, which is a mirror of God's love. To fuel my belief in myself enough to carry out my purpose.

The truth being, I am a leader, but not in the traditional sense. I am a guide and companion for Catholic/Christian women and this is the purpose of my life. For someone so in love with God it would seem easy. But Satan is cunning and works triple time when you decide to work for his enemy.

Hail Mary!
Full of grace
Show me your life
The Lord is with
Me!

She had been standing in the corner of my bedroom next to my nightstand for years. Patiently watching and waiting. The time was now. It seemed like a voice calling. Not one you hear with your ears. One you feel with your soul so that every cell of your being vibrates. My mother's statue of the Blessed Mother, the one in the black and white picture of my mom in her bedroom getting ready on her wedding day, was calling me. "Bring me out of the dust and cobwebs, I am here for you!" the Blessed Mother called to my heart. I moved Her to my writing room.

We began friendship through prayer, extended by my thirst to find out anything I could about her. About what it would be like to be a Jewish woman at that time. About who my friend Mary had been and still is. I began to write about Her, about Her ability to model feminine leadership for us. Her essence drives me to create art inspired by Her beautiful soul and presence.

Blessed art thou
Among women

She reminded me of one of the only things I can remember my mother telling me. It was the most important message Mom needed me to hear about being a woman. It was her response during our conversation about women's liberation. She said, "I don't need to be liberated. I was liberated when I was born." The message translates now to an inspiration to be who she guided me to be and to carry on in her honor. One other important thing Mom said to me? "To thine own self be true." Straight from the mouth of the girls' high school actress, who always played the male roles in their plays because "They were more interesting."

And blessed
am I
the fruit of your womb

As our friendship grew, Mary reminded me that she was my avatar during my decision to become a pastoral counselor, a crazy, complete career change, taken on with four children and a full time job. How else could I have gone to class at night and worked internships? I had dedicated my thesis to her using the theme of the Annunciation. Her courageous "yes" to whatever God intended for her life had brought me to my own "yes" to a life of journeying with others through their pain and sorrow to healing and joy. Her walk with her son through his sorrows was my walk with my clients and through my own life.

Holy Mary
Mother of God
pray for us
who sorrow
who weep
who reject
and bring us
to you and your Son
at our end

So did I really want to be a nun? No. But memories of Bernie found me searching for the book of my elementary school days. I found it. It came lovingly encased in a handmade, blue fabric book cover with a ribbon closing. I voraciously read that same night. As I finished, tears were streaming down my face and neck, sobs heaving my chest.

In reading the book again, at this time in my journey, I realized I had not wanted to be a nun. What I wanted was to live a life in love with God! That was what Bernie had represented to me. I wasn't missing anything. I had been blessed generously with both my husband and God!

The pains of my younger years had fooled me into thinking too often that I was not "good enough". Good enough for anything. Especially not good enough to be heard or to even have a message worth listening to. The pain seeped deep inside and I had become the pain. How could a person so flawed, so ugly, so "fat", so not good enough, be allowed to have a wonderful love affair with God?

Mary corrected my vision of myself. She guided me back to the path of real life while I was running after false gods. I was so stubborn! My search for an illusion ended. My purpose was already there and alive. To guide other women into to the most fulfilling relationship they will ever have. One with Christ, the son of Mary. I have what I have always wanted. I have what I need. She brought me back to reality and reality is good. I am grateful.

Only tears of joy
I cry
For you
my Heavenly
lover

Amen.

Ellen Marie Dumer, LCPC *Helping you bring your 'Feminine Genius' to light… As the first generation of women to come into our wisdom years after being raised in or coming into the Post Vatican II Catholic Church we are ready for the outpouring of the spiritual gifts and natural talents we have been cultivating as we have become mature women of faith. We can work together on an individual basis to design a personally tailored program to lead you to living a Christ-centered and joyful life.*
http://www.livingyourexceptionallife.com/

Part Three

I AM Renewed

"little by little,
as you left their voices behind,
the stars began to burn
through the sheets of clouds,
and there was a *new voice*
which you slowly
recognized as your own,
that kept you company
as you strode deeper and deeper
into the world,
determined to do
the only thing you could do

— Mary Oliver

Story Ten

My Journey Home

Kristen Rockenbach

"The end of all our exploring will be to arrive where we started and know the place for the first time." T.S. Eliot.

The morning mist still hung over the woods the way sleep clings to the eyes of those who are not quite ready to awaken. The dirt path is damp with the rain from the night before, while the leaves that fell last fall outline the journey forward. In the distance there are the sounds of a murmuring brook making its way to the Chesapeake Bay. As I breathe in, my lungs absorb the moisture that hangs sweetly in the air. My mind drifts to how far my journey has brought me and who I have become.

I began to write this story over a year ago. It was about half written when my life shifted focus to the mother archetype. I put this story on the shelf and began to write about my journey to become a "mother" to my 16-year-old nephew. It was a year of learning to live in the divine feminine energy of the Mother; the grace, the ease, the fluidity. Now I return to complete my story a different person than I was before the yearlong journey into and with the divine Mother.

As a young girl and teenager, I spent my summers at the Aloha camps in Vermont. With my summers away from "normal" life, TV, friends, and parents I was allowed the freedom to explore who I was and what made my heart sing. I was surrounded by feminine leaders; each leading in their own way. It was my annual reset that allowed me to reconnect to nature and the divine feminine in me. This was the place Judith Duerk speaks of in the Circle of Stones.

> *"How might your life have been different if there had been a place for you? A place for you to go... a place of women, away from the ordinary busy-ness of life...a place of women who knew the cycles of life, the ebb and flow of nature, who knew of times of work and times of quiet...who understood your tiredness and need for rest. A place of women who could help you to accept your fatigue and trust your limitations, and to know, in the dark of winter, that your energy would return, as surely as the spring. Women who could help you learn to light a candle and to wait..."*

I grew older and chose to study in France for the summer instead of going back to camp. Once I missed a summer it just never seemed the right time to go back.

As I matured, I looked for new role models. Being drawn to the sciences, the role models were always of a masculine energy regardless of gender. As a Physics major, I was usually the only woman in my classes. As I surrounded myself with more and more masculine energy, I lost the feminine that I had learned as a child. I lost my connection to true self. I suppressed my divine feminine. I was logical, planned everything out, wanted order, and took action, got things done.

I continued to move more and more into the masculine; it became more comfortable. I took a job as a consultant for a software company. Women were a minority in the department. It was not unusual for me to be the only woman at a conference room table. Through these years I had wonderful male mentors to help me with my career. Then one day it happened; my client asked me out on a date. This really threw me for a loop. I didn't know what to say. How do I respond? Was it even allowed? When I went to my mentor, he could provide no help. This was completely foreign territory for him. I felt I was swimming with sharks. This moment is when I began to see I had emulated men, played in a man's world by the rules made by men. But in this moment there were no man rules for me to follow. In a moment, I was lost not knowing how to act or be.

In my career, I began to recognize being capable didn't always matter. I was treated differently because I was a woman. There were times when I would ask a client a question and he would direct the answer to my male co-worker. I was talked over. I was challenged to prove I "knew my stuff" before my ideas and recommendations were taken under consideration. In my company I was considered "one of the guys'. I even ate a 48-ounce steak by myself to "fit in" (Let me tell you I will never do that again. I didn't need to eat for 2 days.)

This imbalance grew until one day it hit me. NOW was the time for me to acknowledge and restore the balance of the masculine and feminine within me. Now was the time to do the hard work of realigning and rebalancing myself. As I peeled back the layers I uncovered the messages I received as a child: GET TOUGH. BE STRONG. DON'T CRY. YOU CAN HANDLE IT. DON'T DEPEND ON ANYBODY ELSE. Males were preferred. My parents wanted a boy instead of a girl. No wonder my masculine side took over. "He" is overworked and tired from decades of doing.

But how do I embrace the feminine side? How do I learn to live differently? How do I evolve to stand in the feminine while surrounded by the masculine? The answers came to me. I HEAL by clearing the debris from my path that I have lived with for so long and has restricted me like a corset not allowing a full breath. I HEAL my lineage. I HEAL all the stories I was told and told myself. I HEAL by removing attachments which no longer support me or who I have become. I allow myself to transform like the caterpillar into the butterfly. I am spinning my cocoon now with the trust that when I emerge, I will have undergone a complete metamorphosis.

And so began my year journey into the divine feminine. Like the caterpillar the journey was painful on a physical, emotional, and spiritual level. I had to take off the rose colored glasses. This meant letting go of relationships, redefining others. Some people supported me, others couldn't understand why I was changing or would want to change.

Like a pendulum swinging, I moved from the masculine to the feminine. 100% all in. As I embraced the mysteries and fluidity, it was difficult to give up structure, order, plans. I went through initiations, mystery schools, opening and developing my initiative gifts. I stepped into the mother archetype with my nephew and as a matriarch in the family. I allowed myself to BE not DO. While in this fluidity of the feminine, my inner masculine fought back with trying to control, being harsh. I kept working. I gave myself permission to be creative and explore BEing. I found that photography and writing were creative outlets that my feminine loved and excelled at. I explored the rhythms of nature, communed with the animals, bathed in the moonlight. All the while my inner masculine fought back with everything he could.

As with any overcorrection, momentum slows, a new equilibrium is found. I have deconstructed the Masculine, lived in the Feminine, and now it is time to have a sacred marriage between them as EQUALS. Weaving together the masculine and feminine to create a tapestry of doing and being in joy and harmony. To honor both and have them honor each other. I needed to fall in love with myself again. The masculine holding space for the feminine to expand and grow as he provides support while the feminine receives the space and support provided.

What does that look like? I still work in a male dominated field and prefer it that way. Now I speak from my heart center with all of my clients and colleagues. I push others to explore their feminine. I challenge the traditional thinking. I share all my observations to anyone who asks or is interested and wants to listen. I call upon angels and guides before meetings. I try to connect with the client's higher self so that the deliverables are inline with what they want and need. As a friend of mine says "I came out of the broom closest." I started tweeting inspirational photos and messages that are linked to my Facebook and LinkedIn account. Now everyone can see who I am and what I am doing.

As I step into my new life, I take the positive aspects of my time in a masculine world and apply them from the heart, learned during my journey into the mother archetype. Through this journey was born a new venture to bring heart and soul back into corporations by influencing leaders to leave a legacy of joy and equality.

The drumbeat of mother earth brings me back to the present. The rising sun is starting to glisten off the moist leaves of the canopy above as patches of sunlight filter to the forest floor. I take a deep cleansing breath as I begin my journey home.

Kristen Rockenbach lives outside of Washington DC with her husband and two dogs. She founded Tuckahoe to bring heart and soul back into corporations and to support the health and vitality of the companies and the people that make them up. Tuckahoe helps organizations and individuals realize their potential to thrive by influencing leaders to leave a legacy of joy and equality. Kristen holds an MBA in Management Information Systems and BS in Physics. She is an active member in the community, volunteering with Junior League of Washington, University Club of DC, and Pets on Wheels. Follow her on twitter @Krockenbach www.TuckahoeLLC.com

Story Eleven

Following My Heart:
A Reinvention Story

Krista Riddley

"Every time I release something from the past, I make space for something new and wonderful to come into my life".

I guess I've been a leader in different ways all my life, but have never attached that word to myself. I skipped 4th grade, was the co-captain of the cheerleading squad, won piano competitions, and was the first in my immediate family to get a bachelor's degree. At 22 years old, I took off on my own for West Africa – Ivory Coast to be specific, to study for a year. When I got back, I moved to DC and walked the halls in search of a job on Capitol Hill, which I got pretty quickly. I spent two years there, moving up rapidly to a position of responsibility supporting the Congressman on foreign affairs issues. I received a near full scholarship to Columbia

University to study for my Masters in International Affairs. After my MIA, I joined a non-profit relief agency, and was posted to The Gambia, in West Africa. I moved steadily up the ranks and became a Country Director in Niger, then Zimbabwe, running programs worth over two million dollars. I continued to lead work focused on Africa when I returned home, serving in top level decision making positions for two other non-profits.

After nearly 20 years in international relief and development, I gave it all up and started my own business as a fitness trainer and holistic health and wellness coach. While I was overseas I fell in love with bodybuilding as a hobby. I continued my training when I got back to the US and decided to compete. So I put on my bikini and high heels, and placed top 5 in several figure competitions including a 1st place win against competitors who were probably half my age.

I'm 50 now and as I look back I think, "I did that" but are my most productive days behind me? What lies ahead? I feel I'm at a crossroads, smack dab in the middle of a reinvention.

This reinvention has created question after question after question – Can a solopreneur lead? Who does she lead? My life has changed so much in the last 5 years, I'm not sure who I am sometimes or what will make me truly happy. I know that I was born to be mission driven. I wanted to be a nurse when I was a little girl, to help and heal others. Although I had ideas of becoming an interior designer when I went to college, my life took a turn into non-profit work and I never looked back. Until I burned out. What does a leader do when she burns out?

For a while I was in denial – then thought maybe I just needed a change of scenery – and then maybe a consulting job – and then maybe a leave of absence. In the end, it was a complete break that I needed. In both senses of the word "break." So I broke from the only career I'd ever known. A career that had taken me across the world. A career that had allowed me to see and experience things that most people never will. A career that gave me many leadership roles in a predominantly white environment. Staff looked to me for guidance. I managed budgets and created visions and plans. I advocated for those I supervised and those I chose to hire. I felt important and needed and that felt good. Until it didn't anymore.

I guess it wasn't that part that didn't feel good. It was the constant suffering, abuse and sadness that the world I chose to immerse myself in contained. It was the rape, torture, hunger, killing, disaster and sickness that I was responsible for finding a way to abate. I got jaded too, from the blank looks of young Congressional staffers as I described the rebel onslaught on a village, or the plight of women who weren't being protected by UN troops. I started to feel that the "system" didn't really care, or was otherwise too occupied to seek out a solution to the basic problems of a woman in a village far away who can't feed her children or fears for her life. It's hard to cut through the thickness of everyday life here, of problems that seem more pertinent or solvable.

So I burned out. I can't say exactly when but it wasn't an instant – I got less and less interested and perhaps more discouraged about whether I could actually make a difference in those women's lives. It became too much of an uphill battle -- like Sisyphus rolling that rock. And ultimately too painful. I felt like little parts of me were injured, but I had ignored the pain for so long. I didn't want to become completely desensitized. It's hard not to, it's a way to survive. Stuff the feelings and do the job.

One day my immediate supervisor and the organization's Vice President invited me in for a meeting to talk about taking on new responsibilities and getting out more. We talked for a little while, and then, in his own warm and fuzzy way, the VP said, "How *are* you doing?" And before I could even think, I said, "Burned out."

Whoa. Where did that come from? I suppose from my heart. It was time to go. My journey had begun for a second career.

I have always just followed my head (and heart) to the next challenge. Setting goals, yes, but also letting things flow naturally. When I decided I didn't want to major in interior design anymore I took some classes and discovered a love for African social, political and cultural history. I moved in that direction. When I lived overseas, in a succession of African countries, I was happy and content until I wasn't. And when I wasn't, I decided to move on and return home. When I realized that I had an opportunity to do something that scared me and challenged me, taking a short-term position that had no guarantees, and to let go of a company I felt didn't value me, I did it. And when one day I blurted out "I'm burned out," I knew it was time to go and I did.

What's different about this crossroads I'm on is that it doesn't seem as smooth. Or perhaps I remember the other transitions as smooth in retrospect, but they really weren't at all. Everything I've done has brought me to this moment.

Not that I've found the answer yet – if there is one – but I've finally decided to let go. The light is creeping in through the clouds. I'm reminded of a quote. "When I stop struggling, I float. It's the Law." I'm letting go of the struggle… again. What I think has been so hard about letting go is that it has felt like a failure rather than just a moving on, a natural progression, a response to learning more about me and what makes me tick. Turning the page to the next chapter.

This year has been challenging and has stretched me in new ways. Ways I hadn't expected. I rebranded myself and narrowed my target market to serve obese and overweight Black women looking to change their lives. I felt I was moving ever closer to what resonated and what felt purposeful and authentic. I thought I had figured out how I wanted to serve the world in this iteration. As I pursued my new mission, more was revealed, and things happened that might be called serendipitous by a less spiritual person. One friend called those "God winks." I love that.

Not long after I had completed my new website, I was sitting at my computer and a totally unexpected email came in. A medical doctor at a local practice wrote me saying she had found me on the internet when she was looking for a culturally appropriate speaker to come to her practice and present on wellness to her predominantly black staff. That was truly a God wink. Then, I shared my new focus with an acquaintance, and she told me about a black women's wellness conference that was a perfect fit that was looking for speakers. The kicker was they had extended the deadline because they hadn't gotten enough good candidates. I was accepted to present to that conference and to another one with a primarily black audience. I really enjoyed the energy of working with women's groups and that led me to create and successfully deliver a group weight loss-coaching program. One of the women has lost 40 lbs to date. I served as a coach for participants at two important African American conferences. I reached out more and more to my community. And they reached back out to me.

There were a lot of firsts, a lot of risk taking and a lot of putting myself out there. It was a good thing. But the more I pushed to make things happen on the business side, the more I became aware that I was swimming upstream. What I realized was that while I love the work – the work of supporting women, black women in particular, to transform their bodies and their relationship with food, to put themselves first, to feel better, gain confidence, and become who they really want to be inside and out -- there were too many things I didn't love about entrepreneurship. I had to come to terms with those things and take the next step in my journey.

The biggest challenge for me was the isolation of being a so-called "solopreneur." My entire career, from staffing a Congressman on Capitol Hill, to directing programs in Africa, to advocating for human rights, and finally working to achieve better outcomes for people suffering in disasters and conflict around the world, I have worked with and through others. I excel at the collaborative process of seeing a problem and working to solve it with others – each of us doing our part, and bringing our own unique set of knowledge and experiences to the table to create something bigger. I thrive in that environment, and I miss it – a lot. I miss working towards a mission with the resources available to make big things happen and being with people who share my values and feel as passionately as I do about seeing the vision come to fruition. That is something I haven't been able to recreate in the context of my business, at least not yet. So I want to share my leadership, my passion, my gifts and skills in another way. What this year, and perhaps this 4 years of entrepreneurship has been about, is figuring that out. Leaving and coming back. Learning and growing and coming out stronger and clearer on my path in life.

I've never been so comfortable shining my own light, "bragging" or touting all the amazing things I've done. Even writing that word "amazing" kind of makes me feel uncomfortable. Through my career I've advocated for others, staff, colleagues, poor communities, the abused, forgotten and vulnerable. It feels so natural to do. It doesn't feel nearly as natural to promote myself and my services as an entrepreneur. That has been tough for me. And yet, I know that part of being a leader is letting your light shine, that it's not about *me*, it's about reaching the people I'm called to serve and who need what I offer. For some it's literally life and death. In the final analysis though, I know that what I could bring for those clients, I can also bring to an organization that serves the same demographic, and on a bigger scale than I can do alone.

So where do I go from here? There is a lot of life left to live. A lot of gifts yet to give. So I'll step into my future, and let it take me wherever I can use my skills and experiences to touch people's lives. That's what I've always done. That's leadership.

Krista Riddley is a speaker, writer, award winning figure competitor and holistic health and wellness coach who is passionate about improving the lives of women worldwide. Krista has nearly 20 years of experience in the international development field managing emergency relief, social welfare and anti-poverty programs. She is adept at policy and strategy development, collaborative problem solving, and leading multidisciplinary teams to create sustainable change in people's lives. A creative thinker, Krista writes and speaks nationally and is currently working on a book titled, **"The Soul Sister's Guide to Reclaiming Your Body and Renewing Your Life."** *http://www.kristariddley.com/*

Story Twelve

Trusting and Soaring: All of Me

Monisha Mittal

When I began my community development career in North Philadelphia after graduating college, I became very close with my boss who was twenty years older than me. First a mentor, then a friend, we remain close after 25 years. I wondered…why did I resonate so much with his stories of struggle, coming out as a gay man in a large Irish Catholic family? Why did they feel so familiar? I was a heterosexual girl from a traditional Indian family growing up in America. Why did I feel I understood the terror, the not belonging yet wanting to belong?

You know when you feel different from everyone around you? It's not a conscious thought but something you carry with you. I always felt in danger of not being acceptable as I was and in danger of being 'kicked' out. It took me a long time to understand what made me feel so different and scared.

In fact, this lesson only culminated now, washing ashore, right on time, on the day this story has to be sent to Heal My Voice.

By the time I was eight I had taken to hiding behind the armchair in the living room, for long periods of time. I did it whenever I needed to feel wanted by my mother. I needed her to want me, see me, hug me and make me hers. I wouldn't make a sound. Sometimes I might wait as long as 45 minutes. Inevitably, she noticed my absence and started calling for me. I would wait until I felt truly cared about, and reassured I emerged.

I understand now why I did this. When I was three, my father made a decision that separated me from my beautiful ma for eighteen months to make sure I got the right start in life educationally. By the time I came back, I had forgotten what she looked like and that she was who I missed every day even after I had forgotten who she was. As an adult, my mother has repeatedly told me how much she and my sister cried after coming back from the airport, after leaving me to go back to India to live with my father's extended family. While I could hear her words, I couldn't feel it.

My first night in India, I lay on a separate cot at the foot of the bed where my uncle and aunt lay asleep with my cousins. I remember the distance from my cot to that bed, where all those heads lay together, feeling how they lay knowing they belonged to each other, and me alone and apart. That is when the wound of separateness began. It set a feeling deep down in me that I had not been worthy enough to be kept. I was expendable. This was the story that settled in. It is easy for me to see the underlying anxiety that set in my belly, an underlying fear that I wasn't valuable enough as I was to avoid being sent away and why I was a bed wetter until nearly 10 years old.

What does this have to do with me now? What does it have to do with feminine leadership? It set up a pattern of hiding and waiting for external acknowledgement before feeling safely 'wanted'. I didn't trust myself and hid my true light. I also hid my vulnerability because...I didn't want to be so vulnerable that I needed this love. This completely affected the way I lead. In graduate school, my classmates honored me with a "Class Spirit" award, but specifically called out my "behind the scenes" efforts. In the workplace, I used standards of achievement as camouflage—so those standards became the permission and acknowledgement I needed to feel safer about having room. My fear of 'failing' was so strong that I automatically internalized client and manager expectations as a marker for success. I developed an interesting way of hiding, internalizing expectations, taking on excessive responsibilities to make them happen and setting high standards for myself in the hopes of being seen. I spent 15 years in this pattern and it was exhausting. Yet I rarely felt seen.

By the time I was 11 years old, I started sensing that there might be something different about me. I noticed it in my connection with children. In a new neighborhood, after school, I hung out with four-year old children. I felt at home with their innate openness, their sheer delight and inquisitiveness. It felt so right because they were connected to their heart light. I felt more natural, like my whole self, in these moments. Yet socially I was also aware that I wasn't able to "share" these feelings with my peers in school.

I learned how to listen deeply behind that armchair. Undisturbed by others, I connected to my intuition to make sense of my environment. I learned how to hear not just what was said, but also what wasn't said. I heard a silent language of aspirations, yearnings, fears, sorrow and shame that came from the heart. When my father taught us—math, physics, and religion, he found beauty in the essence of these things. My mother radiated a sweet aliveness and formed her reasoning based on emotional truths and a practical point of view. But I also saw my father use his rational logic to repeatedly squash my mother's way of reasoning and delegitimize her. I saw him care deeply about achieving goals that he believed had purpose and sacrifice the rest of our desires in pursuit of those goals. In the patriarchy we lived in, I watched my mother limit the breadth of her expression to small spaces: making our clothes, dressing us, reviewing our coloring, and singing Bollywood tunes.

So the emotional landscape has always been real to me. I wanted both my father and mother's unfulfilled desires to matter—I also wanted mine to matter. I wanted a leader who understood that despite having less education, she deserved to be lifted up, and that what she had to say was worth listening to. I felt a real leader would understand how to make room for her and learn from her. I also knew in my heart that there was no good reason, no truth, for her to put down. Watching how my mother was treated, the part of me that valued the heart, didn't feel safe opening up.

As I grew, my education encouraged my 'left-brain' intelligences. Outside of literature, there was no place for developing my heart-based intuition. In a competitive business school program, no matter what was said overtly – messages such as 'be all that you can be' and 'follow your passion' and nods to being 'socially responsible'-- it was clear that human-centered vocations such as teaching or social work were less valued and 'low-paying' while careers that lead to money, power, status or other forms of prestige were greatly valued. Numbers were seen as "hard" with jobs in finance being the most lucrative while "feelings" were seen as soft and put down. In college, male friends told me I helped them process emotions. So somewhere they were taught to shut down this piece of themselves. I just hadn't learned how to do that yet. When I fed my heart, volunteering with children at homeless shelters and the children's hospital, I thrived on the emotional connection but wasn't quite sure what to do with my other intelligences.

My worlds felt distinct—institutions with power, capacity and money versus non-profits that cared about humans but had little organizational or monetary resources. And I was scared about not having power myself, not having respect and stamp of 'worthiness' by others: institutions, family, peers. In the institutional and corporate powers I traversed, it especially didn't feel safe to admit the part of my reasoning that was feminine, the part that used emotional intelligence to evaluate a situation and inform my conclusions, or the part that prioritized building up human capacity as an organizing principle. I internalized all of this as a Great Split. I believed I had to choose between my masculine side as a path to 'security' and respect, or a feminine side which felt fulfilling but lead to a more vulnerable, less secure place.

The mistake I made was to believe that I was not powerful just as I was, being all of me. To break free, I had to first understand what was different about me. Working with clients, I used my deep listening skills to fill in the gaps of *what they were saying* to determine *what they really needed* to solve their problem. I organically incorporated the emotional realities of their environment—where people worked well together or didn't—to identify workable solutions. And I included mechanisms to empower their staff where I could. Along the way, an older female colleague pointed out my 'non-linear' thinking as a compliment. This was the beginning of learning how I worked and valuing it.

Then, I had to stop worrying about fitting myself into spaces that were pre-defined by others and too small for me. These spaces showed up in my workplace, in terms of the opportunities available to me. While I received pats on the back for high customer satisfaction scores, no one guessed at the feminine qualities that went into them and I was never seen as someone to develop or promote within the company. The smallness showed up in my personal life, defined in terms of what was expected of me. As it turns out, all of these are examples of giving away my power, because I used other people's determinants to value my worth instead of trusting the power of being my whole self.

This year my way of operating and achieving broke down. The scope of work and number of teams I was overseeing was too large to use my 'touch everything', hands-on approach. My internalized standards became a source of suffering because I constantly saw my failures. I felt my entire notion of success threatened since there was no human way to meet what I expected of me. My leadership role and authority was challenged, also. At one point, I was even verbally asked why I was attending some meetings. It touched my terror buttons of not being valuable enough to keep to the core.

As terrifying as it was, this time something was different. Even though I wasn't sure whether or not I would lose my position or reputation, I knew deep down that my Self was intact and remained inviolate. I had just enough trust that I faced this fear three times until I learned to trust my *own* form of leadership. Rather than react to the challenges from fear (bad mouthing others, feeling like a victim), I found the courage to do what my heart asked of me. I found I had to own the authority and leadership that was being accorded to me; behave as a leader instead of being scared I didn't belong in the role. I made my own judgment calls about how to handle each of the relationships. This also meant I had to find the courage to talk (out loud, oh my god!) to the woman who lead this client's 'trusted' team and sort out the confusion over roles. I wasn't disappointed. I walked away with stronger relationships than when I went in and a profound trust in my ability to handle myself. I also let go of internalizing expectations that didn't serve me—it was too much work. Trusting myself and my own authority, rather than waiting for permission or acknowledgement. These were the lessons from the break down of my leadership style.

Learning to own my power wasn't a process of triumphing over or overcoming anything; this dynamic is also a form of 'dominating' something, which is how society is used to thinking about power. (This gets to why I felt the terror I did. Traditional organizations wield power in a hierarchical way that stresses domination and doesn't consider heart truths. I felt attacked because it dismissed something so innate about me.) Instead, at the depths of my journey, I found a softer power. In a Mary Magdalene meditation, I discovered I had a Divine Mother. I felt her energy as absolute Nurturer, Life-Giver, Healer. She made me feel Safe, deeply loved and cared for. This softness is strong. With this, I trust I belong. Most of all, She gives me the gift of Receiving. I am ok receiving my vulnerability now. In turn, this helps me receive the care, support, and encouragement I wanted but hid from. It is helping me build more authentic relationships with people and money. Relax, Receive, and BE she tells me. In particular, this has meant unlearning 'DOING' and 'ACHIEVING' (yang). I felt this pull the entire time writing this story—constantly needing to shift from 'accomplishing' to 'being' to tell it authentically.

Today I finished a session with my first paid client for my Your Inner Ease business. My services are entirely based on my skills of whole-brain listening. In session, I am filled with EASE and have FUN being my whole self. Also, I learned that being my whole self—which is what I feared the most—*is* the source of my gift for others and the planet. To be all of me, and be in Service, this is how I now define success. I now embrace my unconventional way of seeing and processing the world, its breadth and depth. Now I see, I am BIG and what I have to offer the world is BIG.

It took many hands over the last eight years to increase my sense of safety. With each step, I learned to trust and accept myself more. Michelle James held a compassionate space for me to come out of hiding early on. Andrea Hylen supported me unconditionally as I designed and lead my first whole-brain workshop. At the same time, I participated in a nine-month Priestess process consciously honoring the feminine in authentic connection with other women. I connected with the power of the Divine Feminine in me, which is allowing greater integration of my feminine and masculine expression in the world.

I am coming out. I know the heart has an important role to play in solving individual, organizational and societal problems. My mission is to lead by bringing this heart-logic to the world.

Monisha Mittal's passion is creating high-engagement, collaborative spaces for learning and problem-solving using a blend of techniques—from the traditional to the creative and spiritual. Monisha is pursuing adding body-intelligence based techniques to her approach. Her desire is to serve a greater number of individual clients through www.yourinnerease.com and contribute to better learning and innovation practices in our public and private organizations. She is currently inspired to create panel discussions on feminine leadership in the Washington D.C area where she lives with her husband. Monisha is a proud Board member of Heal My Voice. This is her second published story.

Story Thirteen

Consciously Living and Dying

Karen A. Porter

The first dying process I witnessed was that of my maternal grandmother. In her 90's, Mom Mom had severe osteoporosis and spent her final years in and out of hospitals and rehab centers after breaks and surgeries after various bones snapped during normal movement. She had read the newspaper every day and she was alert and aware until her last two months of life.

When she began to fail, her decline was relatively fast. She was in rehab after shattering her hip and my mother and aunt stayed with her every day and through some nights. When I last saw her, she had difficulty speaking but she was insistent that my mother serve the unseen 'guests' in the room. Mom held her hand and reassured her that she would take care of the visitors.

Even on her deathbed, Mom Mom maintained her practice of hospitality. Whether someone came by daily, weekly or once in a blue moon, she would make her guests comfortable and always serve something to eat and drink.

My mother had been a caretaker for her father, mother-in-law and her mother during their lives and during their dying processes. She had a very different relationship to death and dying than I had. Born in the 20's, during her lifetime it was common for people to die in their homes and be prepared for burial by the family. Bodies were laid out for visitation and viewing in the home. Family members kept a vigil, held a wake and gathered after the burial in the home. Just by attending to the dying Mom learned it was common for the dying to be increasingly in the spiritual realm and less in the physical as the time of death approached. Interest in physical activities like reading, talking, and eating lessened and there was more sleeping, less strength.

Mom Mom died in December, 1999. Three months to the day, Mom received her diagnosis of intraductal breast cancer. Surgery, chemotherapy and radiation only slowed the process. After a recurrence, more chemo and radiation, supplements and miracle herbs were tried. All cancer is horrible and Mom's was especially cruel. She had a complication that allowed the cancer to eat from inside her body to outside. We watched the cancer consume her. Patches of raw red skin decayed and turned black. The places oozed and smelled. It was a very unkind end for a sweet, loving woman.

While my father was Mom's primary caretaker, I assumed the caretaker role too. I found a book on dying consciously, **Final Gifts: Understanding the Special Awareness, Needs, and Communications of the Dying** by **Maggie Callanan**, for Mom to read. She called me, asking that

I bring her labels so she could designate what she wanted to leave to whom. I helped her label her treasures and make lists of who was to receive what. We went through her jewelry and photos. Following a suggestion in the book, Mom wrote a letter to each of us, Dad, her sister, her four children, each grandchild and friends.

To reassure her, ease her mind, I promised Mom that I would take care of Dad. She worried about how he would cope. Married after the war, Mom did everything for Dad including buttering his toast until late in their marriage. After Mom got sick, Dad did a bit of cooking but did not clean or take care of their finances, depending on Mom until the end. He often said that 'the dear lord' would answer his most fervent prayer and take him when he took Mom.

Mom entered hospice care less than a month before dying. She followed the classic pattern of passing, eating less, sleeping a lot, flipping days and nights, losing interest in most things. Her skin grayed, her eyes sunk. She had two episodes of her breathing pattern changing but it regulated. She waited for Dad to accept that there would be no miracle and give her his permission to go. Once he did that, Mom died a couple hours after.

Two years ago, Mom's only sister, our Aunt Pearl entered her dying process. From her first symptom to her passing was only nine weeks. She had an inoperable brain tumor and chose not to pursue any treatment. During those nine weeks, I supported her through the stages, advocating for care, writing letters she dictated and I promised that her wishes would be followed. I made the phone calls she wanted, contacting friends and family. I told her what she needed to hear to help her pass peacefully.

While Dad gave up on living or acknowledging any possibility of pleasure and was ready for 'the dear Lord' to take him once Mom died, Dad's body kept going for eleven years. Dad was a contractor and abused and overused his body for all his working life. He had multiple joint replacements, COPD, nerve damage and multiple fusions in his back and neck, high blood pressure, constant arthritic pain, and had a pace maker/defibrillator for heart issues. What caused his death was liver failure brought on by over use of OTC pain relievers combined with myriad prescription medicines.

Dad's process was rapid. He refused tests and any consideration of hospitalization. When we could no longer transport him to his doctor's office, he was referred to home care. The home care physician examined and interviewed Dad, reviewed his records and since he was adamant about not wanting tests or treatment, referred Dad to hospice care for pain.

Dad was under hospice care for less than a week. Their services were comprehensive and kept him physically comfortable and pain free. My sister, Emily and I were his caretakers. I slept in the chair in the room with his hospital bed. During the last couple days of his life, Dad talked with me more than he ever talked. He asked for and received Last Rites and was ready to pass. He asked me how long it would be. I told him that I did not know, days or weeks. Dad was surprised and asked, "Weeks? That long?"

It was only a few more days. He had been sleeping more, and had lost interest in the physical world. He did not care what was going on, had no interest in music or television and lost all appetite for food or drink. He became more swollen and jaundiced with each day.

Emily had a doctor's appointment so I was alone with Dad when he woke up to tell me that Mom was there and they had been having a discussion. I asked if there was anyone he wanted to see or with whom he wanted to talk. "No," he replied. I asked if there was anything he needed to say. "I love you," was his reply. I told him that all his children loved him and were grateful for everything he had done for us our entire lives. He asked for pain medication and asked me not to leave his side. I held his hand and suggested that Mom was holding his other hand. I said the rosary until well after he fell asleep. Dad never woke up. He slipped into a coma and died less than a day after.

One month to the day of Dad's passing, my younger brother's wife, Peggy, was diagnosed with a very aggressive type of leukemia. She wanted to fight for as much time as possible. Chemotherapy started immediately. Her siblings were tested for a bone marrow match. That first hospitalization was for six weeks.

I spent many of those early days with Peggy. We had a lot of time to talk. Peg had helped so much with Mom and Aunt Pearl and when her sister's husband was dying from pancreatic cancer. She knew the difference and the choices you can make when you have time before an inevitable end that sudden death does not allow. She knew to say what needed to be said.

Even with a perfect bone marrow match, the leukemia did not respond sufficiently to the chemotherapy for a transplant to be possible. Both the leukemia and the chemotherapy wreaked Peg's body. She weighed less than eighty pounds. Treatment focus shifted to quality of life. Her doctor told Peg it was her decision to end treatment and once she stopped, she would have five to ten days, at the most two weeks.

I visited shortly after this news from the doctor. Peg was a wonderful, instinctual cook and she cooked for her family for as long as she could. During this visit, Peg was cooking for the week but also leading Dan through how to cook barbeque. While she cooked and instructed, she talked about final arrangements.

It was during this visit that I told Peg I had wanted to write her a letter at Christmas to tell her that we would always be there for Dan and the girls. Peg said she was waiting for her younger daughter, Mandy, to come home.

During Peggy's treatment and hospitalizations, Mandy, in Missouri for her doctoral placement, came home for long weekends and holidays. She came home for a week-long visit on February 11th. She took her mother to treatment on Valentine's Day. Peg decided that was her last treatment day. She took her last dose of oral chemotherapy the next day and began hospice care the following day. Friends and family came to say goodbye. Mandy notified her work that she would return after the funeral.

Once treatment stopped, and additional pain medication began, Peg began sleeping more. Mandy would report who came to visit while she was sleeping. "They must think I am so rude," Peg said. Always thinking about others, she continued taking care of her family until the end, commenting on the cluttered kitchen table and stopping to straighten the kitchen rug on her way from the loveseat to the bathroom.

Many of us offered to take shifts, or come overnight to help but it was important for Dan, Danielle and Mandy to care for Peg. We supported them as best we could, texting, bringing food, Starbucks and visiting for emotional support.

Her end was long and painful. Peg had hoped for a five to seven day process. She told Mandy it was taking a very long time to die. She stayed on the loveseat, curled up and covered for ten days. Then she went back to her bed. She bled in her brain and behind her eyes, causing both eyes to swell shut and bleed. The blindness caused disorientation and distress when she roused for more pain medication. She bled from her mouth. Her sinuses filled and throbbed with a fungus. Breathing through her mouth parched her throat but she could not swallow so when she tried to drink, water came out through her nose. Peggy died two weeks after she stopped treatment, less than nine months after her diagnosis.

I helped Peggy throughout the process but my more active role was supporting Dan and the girls. I sent a copy of Final Gifts to Mandy and took other copies to their house. I was there the night before she passed. Everyone knew it would not be long. Shared grief, helplessness, distress, comforting, support all mixed. Dan knew it was the end. It was too much to see Peg's suffering. Less morphine more often so she would not choke on the amount of fluid but stay pain-free for the remaining time. Peg died the following morning.

With each process and passing, I came to believe more strongly in personal choice. Dying can be a natural process but the advances in medicine and treatment have shifted the focus from dying in comfort and with some control to living as long as possible no matter the physical, emotional or monetary cost.

Either way, whether a death is sudden or over time, the family suffers. Sudden death leaves a wake of unexpressed thoughts, hopes, fears, wishes and many regrets. Those who pass in time, either short or long, have the opportunity to make their wishes known, make bequests, plan their funerals and say what needs to be said. The price for this is the pain of witnessing the dying and being helpless to change the outcome or lessen the suffering.

I have seen good deaths and deaths which could have been better. Unlike previous generations, we are separated from death as a part of life and succumbed to the fallacy of the power of medicine. Reclaiming dying as a full and natural part of life and supporting our loved ones in a conscious dying process has to happen. It is not an easy process. We cope as we cope with other stresses in our lives. I ate. I gained fifty pounds during my mother's process. I napped. I slept more. I spent money for diversion. With each dying, I grew more aware of the cost on the living and was able to make different choices and take better care of myself each time.

To fight or not, to pursue treatment or not, to decide to manage pain even when doing so may shorten life by minutes, hours, or days, these are our choices to make. Seeing the pain of loved ones during the dying process, my husband, David, and I have talked about having a 'Plan B.' Quick is better. Suffering is horrible for all.

I will continue to support others in their decisions about treatment and quality of life. Inevitably, there will come a situation when I will be making choices about my own end. I am not sure what decisions I will make, but they are my decisions to make. I live by the 'Three R's,' respect for self, respect for others and total responsibility. Taking total responsibility for my life includes the decisions and choices I make in every moment of my life. That will include any decisions I make in the hour of my death. Conscious living includes conscious dying. May we have more awareness and open conversations about every aspect of our lives. May we each take total responsibility for our lives and be supported in our decision

Karen A Porter *is the author of* Live Your Life With Attitude *and* Live Your Life With Attitude Workbook/Journal, *available on Amazon in print and e-book version. Currently the President of the Board of the non-profit organization Heal My Voice, Karen is a contributing author to all the US HMV books. Karen co-authored* Conscious Choices: An Evolutionary Woman's Guide to Life. *Karen is an ordained Minister of Spiritual Peacemaking for the Beloved Community. She practices Sound Massage and leads healing meditations using Tibetan Singing Bowls. Karen is a certified Level 1 Qi Gong Instructor and a Certified Sounds Methods Therapist through the American Institute SMT.*

To learn more about Karen's work or to contact her, visit **www.mamaporter.com**

Story Fourteen

Recovery is Possible

Beth Terrence

"A process of change through which individuals improve their health and wellness, live a self-directed life, and strive to reach their full potential." ~ Working Definition Of Recovery (www.samhsa.gov)

My life has been a journey of recovery. I grew up in a family with severe mental health challenges and active addiction. I experienced extreme psychological, verbal, emotional and physical abuse. How I managed to survive those experiences is a miracle in many ways, but somehow I did. Today, I am able to see the gift in what for many years felt like pointless suffering.

I am a person in long-term recovery. The effects of trauma have been a constant in my life. As a result, I've struggled with anxiety, depression and insomnia as well as chronic health issues. As a teen and young adult, I used substances and emotional eating to cope with my pain. As I tried to muster my way through college it became clear to me that my functioning was affected by my life experiences; my pain was so great it was hard to be present in the here and now.

By my second year of college, I realized I needed help and sought out the support of a mental health counselor provided by my school. This was the first time I found myself being able to open up about some of my experiences. I found this helped me to feel better about life and function better in school. I didn't know it then, but this was the beginning of my journey of healing and long-term recovery.

After college, I entered into a live-in relationship rather quickly, which led to marriage. I found myself in a dynamic similar to my childhood with active addiction and abuse present. I know now this is a common pattern and many people end up in similar experiences to those growing up. It took me more than a decade to begin to pull myself out of the cycle of dysfunction that was all I had known. During that time I went to counseling, I learned self-care, and developed a career as massage therapist and holistic practitioner.

By taking a holistic approach to life and well-being, I found that I was able to live with greater ease, even within the confines of an unhealthy relationship. Still, I found myself unable to leave. As bad as it was, it was nothing in comparison to my childhood. Oddly, there was some comfort in the familiar. I had many of the classic adult child patterns including denial, isolation and shame. I lacked the inner strength, confidence and a strong enough support system to move out into the world on my own.

In 2001, my husband and I relocated and his alcoholism became worse. We moved in with some friends and family temporarily, most of whom were actively using alcohol and drugs. I found myself in a new place, with no support, surrounded by active addiction. My trauma became triggered by this environment – my insomnia, anxiety and fear escalated. I was struggling to maintain my well-being, which I was just beginning to know.

I remembered a friend suggesting that I try Al-Anon or ACOA, but I was always too afraid of what my husband would say or do to go. Now, I felt I had no other options. I went to my first meeting feeling terrified. I just sat and listened. I did this for several meetings. And then, I cried; I began to cry a lifetime of tears. What I heard in those rooms was my story. I learned that I was not alone in my experiences; and others who had similar ones had gone on to live full and happy lives through recovery.

I learned about the 12 steps. I came to understand addiction as a family disease. I got a sponsor, joined an intensive ACOA family group and began to heal. I gathered recovery tools and built a support system. For the first time in my adult life, I began to feel hope for what was possible. I began to move out of the patterns of shame and hopelessness that had kept me trapped in a cycle of trauma and abuse.

I remember the first time I heard something called "The Laundry List" read at an ACOA meeting. I understood for perhaps the first time in my life that others had experienced what I had, too. I say this because isolation is something that occurs for families dealing with addiction and mental health issues. And, as a child growing up in this way, there is no knowledge or understanding that things can be different. We just try to make it okay within the container that we are given - *everything we think, do, and feel is a form of coping.* These are hard patterns to unlearn; seeing and acknowledging them is a first step toward recovery.

Here's "The Laundry List" a.k.a 14 Traits of Adult Children Of Alcoholics, written by Tony A. in 1978 *(Source: http://www.adultchildren.org)*:

1. *We became isolated and afraid of people and authority figures.*
2. *We became approval seekers and lost our identity in the process.*
3. *We are frightened of angry people and any personal criticism.*
4. *We either become alcoholics, marry them or both, or find another compulsive personality such as a workaholic to fulfill our sick abandonment needs.*
5. *We live life from the viewpoint of victims and we are attracted by that weakness in our love and friendship relationships.*
6. *We have an overdeveloped sense of responsibility and it is easier for us to be concerned with others rather than ourselves; this enables us not to look too closely at our own faults, etc.*
7. *We get guilt feelings when we stand up for ourselves instead of giving in to others.*
8. *We became addicted to excitement.*
9. *We confuse love and pity and tend to "love" people we can "pity" and "rescue."*
10. *We have "stuffed" our feelings from our traumatic childhoods and have lost the ability to feel or express our feelings because it hurts so much (Denial).*

11. *We judge ourselves harshly and have a very low sense of self-esteem.*

12. *We are dependent personalities who are terrified of abandonment and will do anything to hold on to a relationship in order not to experience painful abandonment feelings, which we received from living with sick people who were never there emotionally for us.*

13. *Alcoholism is a family disease; and we became para-alcoholics and took on the characteristics of that disease even though we did not pick up the drink.*

14. *Para-alcoholics are reactors rather than actors.*

It was during this time in early recovery that my mother, who had eventually been treated for schizophrenia, died suddenly. I found myself in a period of crisis, loss and grief that was close to unbearable. I thought I had mourned the loss of my mother while she was still alive, as her disease had taken her from me at an early age. But, when she was actually gone, I was able to access the pain and trauma of my life experiences in a much deeper way than I had ever allowed myself to before.

Maybe it was accessing this core wound and going into the depths of my unfelt trauma; or maybe it was the blessing of having a new support system in my life, a "family of choice" made up of folks in my recovery community and my spiritual community that eventually gave me the courage to step out of my marriage. I'm not totally sure; but at 37 years old, I found myself at the beginning of a new journey. I separated from my husband and was finally living outside of a dysfunctional environment for the first time in my life.

It was then that I found my recovery was truly beginning. Now, 10 years later, I am grateful for the life experiences I've had. As painful as they were, I know they've helped to shape me into the person I am today. I am a person in long-term recovery. I have a strong spiritual foundation and have acquired many tools along the way. And, I have the desire and experience to help others find recovery, too!

This desire to help began in 2004, after the death of several friends and relatives from addiction and suicide. I had seen their suffering and was powerless to help. I had also seen and felt the pain of friends and family who were struggling to work through their losses. At this point, I had only a few years of personal recovery experience, but I had also been a holistic health practitioner for 8 years. I knew how important holistic resources were in my own healing and recovery; and I 'd seen how they helped my clients, too. I felt a strong calling to bring holistic tools to those struggling with addiction and mental health challenges.

I contacted an inpatient addiction treatment program in Maryland and volunteered to teach a meditation class. Before I knew it, I was leading clients in a weekly meditation group. This was a great learning experience for me. Although I knew meditation and other holistic resources could be beneficial to people in recovery, I hadn't had much experience with clients in active addiction treatment or early recovery. What I experienced was short of miraculous. Each week, I shared a variety of meditative and contemplative practices as well as journaling and self-reflection.

From the very first day the response was positive. In fact, one young man came up to me after that first group and shared that he'd never imagined he could feel so good without heroin. He felt that meditation gave him the experience of a "natural high" and was excited to have this as a resource in his recovery. Many of the clients reported similar feelings responding to meditation as a powerful tool for recovery.

A few years later, following my desire to bring holistic resources to the recovery process, I returned to school and attained a Certificate in Addictions Counseling. I did two internships and worked for almost two years as an Addictions Counselor Trainee. I was passionate about working in the field, but I found that the role of addictions counselor did not suit me. I felt the "rules" were very uniform and did not support individual client needs. Coming from a holistic perspective of treating the whole person, I found this very challenging.

I really felt that there was a better way I could support people in recovery, but I didn't know what that would be. Although I could bring my holistic approach into some groups, it was limited as I had a very set curriculum to follow and lots of documentation to attend to. Luckily around this time, I had an opportunity to work at a private holistic residential addictions program in Virginia. My role there was as a holistic practitioner and group facilitator. I was even invited to bring Shamanic Healing into individual sessions and groups.

One of the things I learned from this experience was the importance of taking a PEER approach in relating to clients. I found this highly beneficial and key in the effectiveness of my work with the clients in this program. I truly believe that meeting a person where they are, from a place of mutuality and openness is the best way to support recovery and healing.

Recently, I have carried this approach into a program I facilitate at a residential addictions treatment program for women that brings writing, creativity and holistic resources to the recovery process. The focus is to empower clients to reclaim their voices, to become advocates for themselves and to explore recovery tools that work best for them. Reflection, journaling and creativity are powerful tools to support self-exploration and growth on a deep level, especially for people in recovery.

In early 2014, I learned of a new role emerging in the field of Recovery – a Certified PEER Recovery Specialist. I was elated! Finally, I felt like there was a good fit for me to bring who I am and what I have to offer forward. I learned I had less than six months before a grandfather period was ending to complete the training and requirements. My desire to bring holistic resources to recovery was the fuel that helped to catapult me forward in this process.

Through all of the PEER Recovery Specialist trainings, I became more and more excited, as I began to see that there is a strong need for PEER Specialists in our communities. It is a joy to see the emergence of a new Recovery frontier with PEER Recovery Specialists as a key component in supporting change for individuals and families as well as the system of Recovery itself.

PEER Recovery Support offers a gateway onto the path of recovery and an ongoing resource on the road of long-term recovery. I feel strongly that PEERS can engage individuals on the front lines and be a welcoming force that helps to offer a bridge to treatment, services and ongoing recovery support.

There is flexibility in the PEER role that allows for a different type of relationship in recovery – one that really meets a person where they are with equality, empathy and acceptance. It is a person-centered approach rather than systems based one.

My overall goal is to support recovery and wellness; the PEER dynamic allows for that support regardless of circumstances or even a person's willingness. Rather than being judged, rejected or thrown out the door for non-compliance, individuals are met with openness, positivity and possibility.

Here is an overview of some of the support that Certified PEER Recovery Specialists offer:

- *Helping individuals to recognize there are multiple pathways to recovery and wellness*
- *Participating as part of an individual's wellness/recovery team*
- *Helping an individual to identity personal strengths, capacities, talents and skills*
- *Offering their experience, strength and hope strategically to support an individual's recovery*
- *Helping to empower people and families in recovery*
- *Providing a self-directed approach, supporting what the person in recovery wants, not only what the provider wants to accomplish or see*
- *Advocating for the recoveree and helping them to learn how to advocate for themselves*
- *Supporting an individual in experiencing optimism, hope and well-being*
- *Helping an individual to focus on the present – on what they can do today to support and strengthen their recovery*
- *Assisting in goal setting, self-care and recovery planning*

- *Supporting individuals and families from crisis to long-term recovery*
- *Offering a holistic approach to life, well-being and recovery*

Having grown up in a time when there was little or no support for individuals and families dealing with mental health challenges and addiction, I feel passionate about being able to help others have a different experience than I did. My growing up experience was one of extreme abuse, isolation, and abandonment. The denial that pervaded my family and community was detrimental to a child and young adult. No one should have to bear that alone. Today, I believe that there is a potential for a different experience - one that comes from a community approach to Recovery.

I hope to help others know that *RECOVERY IS POSSIBLE*, to find recovery pathways that best serve them and to support an experience of wholeness and well-being for individuals, families and communities. I am excited to begin my journey as one of the first Certified PEER Recovery Specialists in Maryland, to combine this role with my work as a Holistic Health Practitioner and Facilitator and to explore what's possible as we open the doors to a new way of Recovery.

__Beth Terrence's__ vision is to support others in living a heart-centered, balanced and joyful life through discovering the healer within. She is a trained Shaman, Holistic Health Practitioner & Facilitator, Certified PEER Recovery Specialist, Speaker and Writer. Beth believes that her own life journey has served as a catalyst for the message she brings to the world – that at our core, we are all beings of love, light and peace – we just need to "remember".

Beth resides in Annapolis, MD, with her loving partner, Mario and her cats, Massimo and Clover. To learn more, visit **www.bethterrence.com** *or* **www.holisticrecoverypathways.com** *for resources on holistic tools for recovery.*

Section Four

I AM Prepared

We delight in the beauty of the butterfly, but rarely admit the changes it has gone through to achieve that beauty.

~Maya Angelou

Story Fifteen

Leadership Begins with Me

Kathleen Nelson Troyer

For most of my career I have worked as a Human Resources Consultant with several technology start up companies. I help them recruit and retain talent. The thing about start up companies is that the infrastructure and support isn't there yet; it is being built, or "started up". This creates a unique work environment where people are hired to do one role, but often wear many hats because that is what the company needs.

The successful companies I work with have leaders who know how to inspire and harness the power of the team to align with the company's vision and mission. The best leaders have clear boundaries. They are willing to get in the trenches with the entire team. They lead by example and are willing to jump in and do the dishes and empty trash cans. Everyone knows who these leaders are and their place is decision making. There is no confusion. However, they don't lead from a pedestal, but arm-in-arm with everyone at the company.

I have been lucky to work with some amazing leaders and others who weren't as effective. It is inspiring to be in the presence of a great leader. From the less effective leaders, I learned what not to do, which is equally as valuable.

I joined the *Heal My Voice Feminine Leadership Project* back in early 2013. At the time, I was running my own HR consulting company and was also a partner in a collective coaching start up. In January of the same year, I attended a women's leadership conference with my three business partners. We had been working together for over a year to launch our coaching and training company. We lived in different parts of the country and were building our company virtually. We spent hours on the phone, especially in the beginning. We put a tremendous amount of thought and intention into how we would work together and our vision for the company. With four owners, and several founding members, one of the biggest challenges was finding consensus. In total, we were a group of 27, all with different life and professional experience levels and all with different methods and opinions. Getting the entire group into a place of alignment was a huge challenge. Looking back, I see more clearly that getting 27 people on the same page was nearly impossible and the way we structured the leadership of the company further confused things.

Before we even agreed on the name of the company, before we set up the corporate structure, we knew we needed some very solid agreements to be effective and for the company to be successful. One of my partners suggested we use the Co-Creators Agreements. This list of agreements is based on the writings of Barbara Marx Hubbard, a conscious evolutionist. These types of agreements stand as a base for many conscious groups and organizations. This was my first exposure to an evolutionary business model. I was excited about the prospect of experiencing Co -Creator Agreements to build a business in a purposeful, conscious manner. We developed vision and mission statements and added our Co-Creator Agreements into the company policies. The four owners intended to show up as leaders and share our unique gifts to help our clients and our members (coaches) do the same in their lives. It was a beautiful concept that required a fierce commitment to our vision, mission and our agreements.

I learned so much about myself and my own leadership style during this time. In August of 2012, about nine months in, I was having some health issues and had turned to a holistic chiropractor and health coach for help. She suggested I do some comprehensive functional tests. When the tests came back, they showed I had developed extreme adrenal exhaustion. The following six months were both emotionally and physically challenging for me. Thankfully, I had a great team of holistic professionals who helped me take care of my body, mind and spirit. I had to put my own self-care first. That began with making sure my body had enough rest - at least 8 hours of sleep at night and a nap whenever I felt tired. I also carved out "white space" on my calendar every day; time for me to do whatever I wanted and needed most. My white space might be more sleep, a walk, a trip to the spa or a chat with a friend.

When I think back on this time, I clearly see that I put all of my energy into this coaching company. I found myself deferring to my partner's preferences for the greater good of the company. There were many times when I had clarity on how to navigate a certain situation, but ended up compromising for the sake of the collaboration. There were times when the decision of the group didn't feel aligned to me. If the four of us weren't aligned, what chance did the company have to grow and become successful? I found myself spending hours every week in meetings that went nowhere and solved nothing. Too much time in meetings, and not enough time getting things done, is not a good way to run a company and it's stressful. Once a decision was finally made, we struggled with execution. There was a continual cloud of fear hovering over us as we were sensitive about potentially upsetting one of the partners. In retrospect, I see how draining this was for me. It was impossibly exhausting juggling the needs of 27 people while making business decisions. By the time the four of us came together in person for a leadership conference, it was clear to me that I needed to re-evaluate my role in the company, especially considering my health concerns.

For all our technology wonders like Skype and free cell phone calling, getting together, face to face with my partners, was necessary. It, like other decisions, was difficult to gain a consensus. I had to push for us to meet in person because I hoped that we would gain inspiration from the conference and that could help us strategize the company's next steps. Three of us were on the same page and one of the partners felt it was more important for her to network and meet new people. Instead of working together during the lunches and evenings as we intended, the lone wolf decided to join the VIP conference and have meals and extra "bonus" conference content. All of this meant time away from the group of four. I was frustrated because I had high hopes for our time together considering we started a company together without a physical meeting. As much as I wanted the four of us to share the same vision, it was apparent that was not the case and might never be the case. I realized that even though we had very clear agreements when it came to the company statements, it came down to our own personal interpretation of those agreements. That was one of the biggest lessons I personally learned. It isn't enough to have agreements, you have to talk about what the agreements mean to you and your business partners. You have to have a clear understanding of everyone's place, duties and a process to solve issues.

Within a month of that conference, I resigned my ownership and walked away from the company. It was an aligned decision but it was also painful. I put so much time and energy into this project. It had become part of my identity. Being part of the core team who gave "birth" to the company, it felt like I was giving up my baby. My father told me when he and my mother divorced that he needed me to understand that in order for him to maintain his self esteem, he had to leave the marriage to my mom. At the time, I didn't really understand what he meant, but I thought about him as I made my decision to leave this company. It was one of Life's "a-ha" moments.

Before leaving the company, I did some serious soul searching and asked my partners to re-align with the agreements we had made. Communication is key in any relationship, especially with business partners. Most of the requests I made had to do with communication. I knew when I made the request that there would be two possible outcomes: I would stay or I would go. I spent hours crafting an email, taking great pains to be as clear as I could about the challenges we were facing as a company, and asked for a re-commitment to the agreements we made when we began. In the email, I took complete responsibility for myself and did not blame anyone. I asked for a meeting as soon as possible. I knew when I sent the email that I was taking a stand for my own integrity and my own leadership. I wanted us to all re-align and knew that I would have to go if we were not able to do so.

I sent the email on Monday. Two of my partners reached out to me and told me they supported my request. One of those two told me that my request was simply a restatement of our previous agreements. The third partner lashed out claiming that beneath the surface of my requests was a push for "new rules". I knew, for my part, my request was coming from a deep place of wanting this to work for all of us. Although somewhat typical of the dynamics, it was still upsetting.

By Thursday of the same week, it was clear that we were not going to be on the same page today nor in the future. I called the partner I felt closest to, and shared my decision to leave. She told me she recently decided to leave the company as well. She also told me I was being too nice and wasn't clearly telling the challenging partner what I thought and how I felt about working with her. I took that feedback to heart and made a vow to myself to speak my truth plainly.

On Friday we met again as a virtual group and two of us resigned. I told the challenging partner that it was difficult to work with her because her actions did not match her words. I told her I didn't feel that she walked her talk. As I spoke, I felt the blood race through my veins and my heartbeat accelerate. My voice shook with emotion during that conversation. I knew at the time that I was acting in a way that was aligned and congruent with myself and my beliefs and my needs, no matter how difficult the path was. In that moment, I knew I was acting as the best leader I could be. Life can be messy sometimes and it is in those times that we have the opportunity to lead with guts and grace, even if our voice shakes and our heart breaks a little.

I look back on the whole experience as a profound learning opportunity. It was hard to leave the company I co-founded. I poured my heart and soul into it and visualized future hopes and dreams for it, just like you do for your child. Hindsight is often better than 20/20 vision. I now see that the signs of challenges ahead were there from the beginning. We had one partner who spoke about being a leader every third sentence and was a self proclaimed "visionary". I believe that a leader should lead by example and let her actions speak for themselves. One person doesn't get a monopoly on being visionary simply because they believe it to be true. I believe all four of us are visionaries and we all did our best to lead ourselves and the company. Being unwilling to have bare-bones uncomfortable conversations was one of the downfalls of our partnership. The other partner who left and I were willing to do that, and as a result we were seen as "difficult".

Projecting the two of us as "difficult" upset me and didn't feel fair, but this is what I have learned since then: When you step up as a leader and speak your truth, you make yourself a bigger target for other people's projections and their own personal insecurities. The world is truly a mirror. Whether or not we choose to see it that way, does not make it any less true. People project their emotions, insecurity, ego, anger and happiness all the time in this world. A leader understands this and is strong enough to hold her own in the face of random projections. I believe that a good leader is willing to have uncomfortable conversations in a fair way, admit when she is wrong and keep moving forward.

I don't regret being one of the founding partners of the company. I am grateful I maintained my own company during this time because it supported me financially while launching the coaching company. I clearly see now that I took on too much running my own company and launching a new company; so much so that my health suffered and I developed adrenal exhaustion.

The past year and a half I have been focusing on my health and refilling my "tank". I did this by putting my self-care first. Now I am very careful who I collaborate with. In order for a collaboration to be effective, there needs to be mutual respect and the desire to listen, understand and effectively communicate. There must be a willingness to move beyond any issues that come up and to resolve them fairly and openly. Being part of a successful collaboration means taking full responsibility for your actions, but also being willing to admit mistakes as they come up. Mistakes are some of the best learning opportunities. I make it a point in my business to allow for them and learn from them.

One of the biggest bonuses from this experience was taking a look at my own personal and professional boundaries. I see how my issues around acceptance and approval impacted the outcome. I believe that we do the best we can with what we know at the time. As we learn more, we make better decisions - we add more tools to our toolbox, which makes us more masterful architects of our lives. What I know for sure is that leadership begins with our relationship to ourselves. We are all leaders of our own lives.

Leadership begins with me.

Kathleen Nelson Troyer is the founder of Gently Moving Forward and CEO of Jigsaw Staffing Solutions, Inc. She works with organizations and individuals as a human resources consultant, trainer, coach and mentor. She has been studying human potential, psychology and transformation for the past 25 years. She holds master level certifications in coaching, NLP, and Ericksonian

Hypnosis. She leads intensive individual and group retreats and facilitates family and systemic constellations. Kat lives in a seaside cottage with a magical garden about 25 miles south of San Francisco near Half Moon Bay, California with her fabulous husband John, their three cats and dog.

www.gentlymovingforward.net

Story Sixteen

Now is the Moment

Charlotte Rudenstam

In the middle of a 21-day dynamic meditation challenge, in the second phase, catharsis, I suddenly saw the word *The JoyRide* in front of me, written in letters made by *fire*. I found a pen and wrote it down. It felt crucial, and I was certain that I would forget it if I didn't note it immediately. Walking out of my green meditation room, I went into our office and said to my husband: "I have the name. We are going to call it the joyride."

He did neither cry out of joy nor dismiss it. He was rather considering it. I was jumping up in excitement beside him. "I found the name, I found the name, and this is it!"

Some hours later he said, "Yes, you are right. The joyride it is."

This happened in October 2013. The joyride was born. I gave birth easily to what I didn't really know at the moment, more that this would be the name of what we were about to create together.

Alexander and I had worked – and been lovers – together for more than a decade. From the very start we knew that we would create something great together. We wanted to help people transform from a state of fear to a state of love. Both of us had long inner journeys, uncovering deep truths about ourselves, and me feeling, now and again, in contact with my pure essence.

As I went further on this inner exploration, I realized the importance of my sexual energy. It is powerful and I became aware of my drive to share this with the world.

So we started leading groups and we were kind of borrowing another person's trademark organizing festivals where sexual energy was included. Now, in 2013, it was time to break free of other people's energy, to give birth to something, that purely was created and flavored by us. When this name, *The JoyRide*, came flying to me from my sub conscious, I knew we were there.

I just loved the metaphor. Life as a joyride, life filled with love, sex and freedom. I saw pictures of joyrides, I saw that the joyride could picture what I want life to be: An invitation to feel it all, the ups, downs and the stillness in between, the worries, the laughter, the sexual energy, the grieving, the fears, the shame, the playfulness, the compassion, the whole lot.

Some days later during another cathartic moment in the dynamic meditation, there came one more word. I got *The JoyRide Experience.*

What I didn't know at the time was that this summer I would live thru an amazing experience, where I sometimes questioned the wiseness of being guided by my inner voice. There were moments when it felt like I would die from this experience. And there were moments when I felt that my whole life had been a preparation for this specific experience.

When being in the midst of an emotional thunderstorm, I took a meditative ride with my bike, thru a Malmö dwelling in the sort of laziness a heat wave creates. The thunderstorm was happening within me, and outside was the sunny city, with happy people being free to go to the beach. I was in a totally reverse universe, giving myself space to go for a short swim and then back to work, back to the chaos, back to the gruesome situation, back to what seemed to be Hell.

And then, while biking in the summer city, being surrounded by flowering trees and the smell of freshly cut grass from the neighboring lawns, I had an epiphany. I remember exactly where I was when it happened, just a minute from our little townhouse, the railway to the right and all the trees to the left and me and the golden bike on the gravel walk in between.

The epiphany was this: *My whole life has prepared me for this situation.* I have gathered knowledge, experience, information, strengths, guts, inner space, grounding, a sense of value, just to be able to meet this thunderstorm standing on my two feet. Standing and embracing it, instead of fleeing it, breathing thru and being curious about what the next moment will bring, instead of going into shock, instead of feeling sorry for myself.

In this moment it was possible to see all the tools I have gathered to be able to stand in my feminine leadership this very day.

And I felt gratitude.

I felt gratitude for life paradoxically being so kind to me.
I felt gratitude for all the experiences I have had thru life.
I felt gratitude for me finally being able to embrace the totality of being Charlotte.
I felt gratitude for the awareness of some of the tools in my toolbox.

I could remember that I, more than once in my life, have thought: *I will learn this to use later. What I am doing now is a rehearsal to something that is going to happen later.* And now was that later.

I understood the meaning of being bullied as a child, of choosing to be a journalist, becoming chairman of a parent-run daycare center, writing a book on public speaking, being afraid and than meeting different fears, and of doing this huge inner journey, of being in contact with my body and not just being a talking head.

And now it was time to be an executive. To be the leader. To act in the moment. To be in peace with the experience. To actually be curious about what the next step in life would be. To be able to stand in total acceptance of surrender to what is, of having no control, of being in the flow, of meeting life, dance with life, instead of trying to control it.

In February 2014 we signed a lease with a foundation running a children's summer camp. We would rent the place for a week to create our love festival *The JoyRide Experience* on the premises. The chairman was aware of who we were, and what we intended to create at the place.

I had a gut feeling from the beginning. A gut feeling that something might happen even though we had the signed contract, It seemed like there was a yes to us being there, but at the same time there was something in the energy, like a reversing power, because one clause in the contract was that we couldn't name the place in our marketing. We spoke about the risks with the clause, but left it at that.

During the spring we were preparing the festival. We visited the place several times. I began to feel safe.

The slogan for *The JoyRide Experience* is: Life filled with love, sex and freedom to be you. Our aim was to create a festival, where people had the possibilities to meet their fears, and try to act in new ways. A festival with a big heart, plenty of spirituality and totally drug free. A festival filled with dance, breathwork, tantra, meditation, qigong, dao and with a possibility to explore sexual energy.

In early summer, I was at the train station in Berlin. A bit stressed, we were looking for the track to our train. Suddenly my phone was ringing. A voice on the phone says she's a journalist and wants to ask some questions. I answer them, and since I have worked as a journalist for ages, I am very aware of which words to choose. Two days later my husband has the chairman of the summer camp in his ear. She wants to break our lease. The reason is that a local newspaper has written about our "sex festival".

In a way it's like we are living in our vision. We wanted to create a festival, where it's possible to meet fear, shame, and shock – and what we meet, what we experience, is just that. It's like the fear is a fence, which prevents love from entering. We had not, in our wildest dreams, imagined that fear would throw us out of our own love festival.

We were in the middle of June now, and my husband met with the chairman, and after the meeting everything was okay. We had a couple of jumpy, nervous days, until the matter was settled.

A month later there is another article in another newspaper, mentioning the festival, and linking it to nudity. Two days later my husband receives an e-mail saying that the venue has withdrawn our contract. This happened three weeks before the start of the festival. We had worked for more than six months with the project, we had gathered workshop leaders and participants from several countries, and now ... nothing.

For a moment it felt like fear was the winner. It felt like our aim to bring more love to the world was crushed.

And in a flash, suddenly there were reporters everywhere. We were asked if we were planning on suing the place. Frantic question: What happens now? We were able to be calm in the middle of the thunderstorm. At the beginning of the week the media called the festival a "sex festival", and some days later it was referred to as a "love festival".

A whole week passed, when it was impossible to promote the festival because we didn't have a venue. A whole week while we were searching for alternatives. My husband went to a meeting, hoping that we would get an agreement where we would receive compensation for their withdrawal of the lease. We knew that we had not broken the contract and that the only reason they broke it was fear.

My husband came back from the meeting empty handed. The worse had happened. We had no festival, no money, a lot of debts, no income – and a lot of people cheering us, hoping for us to find a solution. During this thunderstorm, love was flooding towards us. People gave us lots of ideas, and even some money to support us, and the media coverage made the festival known to many people.

I knelt down next to our bed. I was crushed. I see us losing our home. I imagine our little company going bankrupt. I was at the bottom. I lay naked on the bed. I lay there for more than an hour on a beautiful summer evening in the midst of a heat wave and something in my heart transformed from desperation to curiosity. What would happen now?

I entered our office, sat down naked in front of my computer, and then a miracle. My husband says: "What if we create the festival in the middle of Malmö? What if we ask Paul at Tangopalatset?" It took me a minute to reply – and then I said: "Yes, phone him immediately".

It was now only two weeks before our *JoyRide Experience* was supposed to start.

Two days later we had created *The JoyRide Malmö – love in action*. A smaller festival. A shorter festival. A love festival in the middle of Malmö. In the festival space I had the possibility to *be* in totality. To be the festival queen. To not worry about the bills we would have to pay later. To just be in my loving presence.

I had an epiphany in the middle of the week when we still hoped there would be *The JoyRide Experience*, and some days before *The JoyRide Malmö* was born. That epiphany helped me thru the experience and into love in action. During those four days in Malmö, creating our love festival I was really in tune with my life force energy and I knew that everything was exactly as it was supposed to be.

Today, weeks after the festival has happened, I feel humbled by my own force. I feel humbled by the fact that I had the power to be the energetic heart of the festival.

Some years ago, I created an exercise, where at the end I was standing in the middle of a circle showing my life force energy to the people surrounding me. The words were: *I am a life embracing power engine.* Today I would add, that I know what the power engine consists of. It's my sexual energy. It helps me find the depths of myself; helps me get in contact with my inner guidance; helps me be grounded.

As a *life embracing power engine* I meet the world. Embracing love, embracing life, embracing freedom to be me, and embracing me in my feminine leadership.

Charlotte Rudenstam works as a writer and coach focusing on relationships and sexuality. She arranges trainings, groups and festivals within The JoyRide concept. Love is my religion, states Charlotte, and her passion is to spread words of love, sex and freedom to the world. As a coach, Charlotte meets her client in total presence, and has the ability to inspire her clients to live their potential, including their sexual energy. She lives in Sweden. Be inspired by Charlotte in her blog lustochliv.blogspot.com (some blogposts in English), www.charlotterudenstam.se, www.thejoyride.se You can reach Charlotte thru social medias like Facebook, Twitter (Lustochliv), Instagram. Email: charlotte@lustochliv.se

Story Seventeen

Leadership Rx

Kym Erickson Martin

Cancer is my leadership story. Like beacons in a sea of darkness, my most valuable leadership lessons emerged once the fear of each of my three cancer diagnoses subsided. My cancer journey began in 1983 – the month following my seventeenth birthday – and spans across three distinct stages of my life. Whether I am aware of its presence in each moment or not, cancer shapes my view of the world.

The late medical pioneer, Dr. Tom Ferguson, coined the term "ePatients" to describe "individuals who are *equipped, enabled, empowered* and *engaged* in their health and healthcare decision." (Ferguson, Tom. ePatients: How They Can Help Us Heal Healthcare. White paper, 2007. **http://e-patients.net/e-Patients_WhitePaper.pdf**)

Internet leveled the imbalance of power and accelerated a patient's ability to access medical information anytime, anywhere. ePatients are active participants in their health who work as partners with physicians to rise out of the subordinate role patients historically played.

I am an ePatient.

Engaged, educated, equal and *empowered* best describe my unique ePatient strengths. I *engage* fully in my medical care, practice a higher degree of self-care, and assume ownership of my personal health. I *educate* myself via credible online resources, certification programs and meaningful conversations with other patient peers to craft well-informed questions about my conditions. As an *equal,* my physicians are partners in assessing my treatment options; they know that I ultimately decide on my medical plan. *Empowered,* I confidently move forward with the care option best suited to my needs, preferences and goals.

Every woman, man and older child in need of healthcare can and should act as ePatient leaders. If you also play the role of family caregiver, where you care for young children, aging parents or both, please apply the principles above and leadership prescriptions (Rx in shorthand) below to step out as an eFamily Caregiver and take the lead on behalf of your loved one's medical care.

Leadership Rx #1: Let Go

I vividly recall pivotal moments of peace, when my cancer experiences brought clarity to my otherwise tumultuous life. As a teenager, my naiveté in grasping the gravity of my Hodgkin's Lymphoma diagnosis was a gift, as was the cancer itself. I was on a destructive path, consumed with anxiety and relentless family drama, with which I coped by slowly killing myself with alcohol, nicotine and caffeine in my paradoxical attempt to survive. My immune system collapsed under the toxic assault and cancer took hold. Then cancer saved my life.

Chronic, dry cough and fatigue are classic symptoms of Hodgkin's Lymphoma, which I easily ignored as a sleep-deprived teenager with a pack-a-day habit. Unexplained lumps in my neck that popped up overnight, coupled with increasing fits of numbness in my right arm weren't so easily ignored.

A lymph node biopsy confirmed my fate. My doctor delivered the news of my Hodgkin's Lymphoma diagnosis with great compassion and deep concern for my emotional well-being. My parents, unprepared for the worst, left for home to fetch an overnight bag so my mother could stay and watch over me until morning. I shuffled back to my hospital room in a daze of blurred thoughts. In my fear-filled solitude I gently cried and spoke this prayer aloud, *"God, I know this is going to suck. Please give me what I need when I need it, and give me more when I need more."*

My faith ignited before I spoke the last word as my all-encompassing request for patience, courage, strength, stamina and recovery brought a palpable sense of calm that slowed my pulse, dried my tears, and humbled my ego. My prayer sustained me through heart-wrenching phone calls to break my news, three significant surgeries, forty rounds of radiation therapy, and plentiful stares from my teachers and friends on my first day back as a senior in high school. I radiated the peace of God and a sense of health that no one – not even I – expected.

With absolute certainty, the most impactful leadership prescription I internalized from my Hodgkin's Lymphoma experience was to let go of my fears and trust in God, whatever the outcome. The thought of death did not occur to me as I believed my experience was intended to set me straight and to keep me from jeopardizing God's plan. That is, until I caved in to the fear of being teased or taunted about my faith in God and I slowly let go of His hand. Though I carved out a successful path into adulthood despite my transgressions, I live with great regret knowing that I inflicted and endured senseless emotional pain and anxiety because I held on to fear and let go of God for nearly thirty years.

Leadership Rx #2: Listen and Be Heard

My second cancer diagnosis arrived in 2004, when I was thirty-eight and our only son was three years old. After stepping out at the peak of my technology sales career, I settled into life as a stay-at-home mom. Managing our family's move from Connecticut to Maryland required I was current on my litany of doctor appointments before we crossed state lines. My dermatologist, the last doctor on my list to see, only had availability on our scheduled moving day.

My repetitive exposure to radiation therapy and years of subsequent follow up chest x-rays, mammograms and CT scans caused changes in the pigmentation of my skin that required bi-annual mole exams and frequent self-checks. I discovered my first suspicious mole in 1992 and my dermatologist blurted, "If I don't remove this mole, it will kill you." Vigilance became my mantra and I have since had sixty or so suspicious moles removed, several of which were precancerous.

So on that day in 2004, the mole in question was new, dark and, I believed, aggressive. Because it was the size of a pinhead, my doctor said, "Kym, I don't think it's anything to worry about." To which I replied, "I do. And you need to remove the mole today. As soon as I leave your office, I am moving to Maryland and don't know when I'll connect with a new doctor."

My dermatologist, a self-proclaimed "doctor to the stars" of Greenwich, dismissed my request one last time before he surrendered. Within minutes, the mole was excised, bottled up, and labeled for testing. He called our new home the following week and claimed it was a good thing "we" found it early: melanoma *in situ*, a self-contained, early stage form of the dreaded skin cancer. I hate to think how that mole might have progressed if I accepted my doctor's arrogance rather than listened to my own intuition, which today I believe was God nudging me to persist.

The primary leadership prescription I embraced from this brief exchange with my dermatologist is to listen closely to my internal nudges and to not allow my doctors to play God. Fear is rampant in medicine, and it can be a monumental task to keep one's wits. Cancer taught me to tune in, listen to what feels true and express my personal needs, preferences and goals – lather, rinse and repeat – until I feel heard.

Leadership Rx #3: Lean and Leap

My true faith walk began July 2011 and is the bedrock of my life today. Early on, I was bathed in God's love, grace and mercy, and giggled with glee as his blessings brought greater clarity to the monotony of my day-to-day existence. I experienced pure joy, peace and love that transcended all of my prior beliefs and understanding of happiness. The warmth of God's presence can only be appreciated through personal experience.

Though baptized as in infant, the concept held no true meaning until I publicly turned my life over to Christ in August 2012, along with our then eleven-year old son, ever grateful that we both appreciated the gift we received through salvation. Two weeks later, a questionable breast MRI and subsequent needle biopsies confirmed that I had breast cancer. Fear threatened to derail my newly affirmed faith, but I remained grounded in the knowledge that my life was safely in Christ's hands.

Still, I struggled to believe God would take my life so soon after I committed. I searched for lessons to learn from the experience so I would be of better use to God from that day forward. Like a neon sign, the words "LET GO" flashed in my mind. Relieved to have spiritually let go of my life weeks earlier, I faced the reality of double mastectomy with breast reconstruction and the need to let go of a central part my feminine physicality. Christ's peace and God's presence enabled me to let go emotionally of the fear looming around my diagnosis.

The cancer was contained to my right breast. After a six-millimeter tumor and the surrounding tissue were surgically removed, I was left with clear margins, clean lymph nodes and only localized skin invasion. Standard protocols in the US recommend chemotherapy for tumors in excess of five millimeters. For a one millimeter differential and minimal skin invasion, I faced six full rounds of chemotherapy and a year of Herceptin, the same regimen offered to women with much more advanced disease. Radiation therapy was ruled out given my treatment history, which left chemotherapy as the only conventional medical treatment available. Against my deepest sense of dread, I agreed for the sake of our son.

But I remained profoundly conflicted. You see, I hold a strong belief in the body's ability to heal naturally and in the power of food as medicine (so much so that my license plate reads "FOOD RX"). Years prior, I pursued my certification as a wholistic nutrition consultant to better manage my risk for cancer recurrence. Despite my passion to use food as medicine, my limited knowledge was simply not enough for me to wholistically manage my breast cancer. So I prayed hard and often for an alternative and natural path to treat my disease.

By the grace of God, my dear friend introduced me to the brilliant and gifted herbalist she had long worked with for her own health. Persistence paid off when my friend secured an appointment for me the day before I was scheduled to have a venous port surgically implanted in my chest for my chemotherapy infusions. During my initial sixty-minute consultation, I learned that my herbalist had dedicated his life's work to the treatment of cancer, with a primary focus on breast cancer. He listened carefully to my history, reviewed my findings, and assured me that he could address all my needs through nutrition and medicinal herbs to reverse my diagnosis. I leapt at the chance.

As I hung up the line, I danced with abandon around the house, sending cheers of praise up to God for His divine intervention, then jumped in my car and set off for a previously scheduled appointment with my oncologist. Spiritually inspired, I asked my oncologist to cancel my port surgery set for 7:00 am the following morning along with my entire chemotherapy treatment plan.

Stunned, my oncologist expressed his disapproval, though he agreed to see me as his patient and engage in a conversation with my herbalist to discuss my care. My internist, more comfortable with my decision to abandon the chemotherapy route, now orders the blood work I require every three months. My herbalist interprets the results, discusses his findings with me via a Skype consultation, and uses those results and personal updates on my wellbeing to refine my treatment protocol.

The impact of my breast cancer diagnosis is foundational to my current leadership journey in healthcare. My experience as a three-time cancer survivor becomes even more compelling when coupled with God's intervention and my choice to design an integrated, wholisitic and personalized approach to my breast cancer care.

Leaning on God, I take leaps of faith that I might not otherwise have the courage to consider. This is the leadership prescription I subscribe to myself on a daily basis. I check in with God throughout the day to stay in sync with His plans and to avoid dramas and distractions as best I can (realizing that at times I am the source of the drama or distraction). Walking by faith, I am reminded of my humanity and, in turn, embrace my humility.

God Reveals

My leadership journey in healthcare is presently unfolding. In June 2013, three months after my final reconstruction surgery, I received my first invitation to speak at a highly-regarded healthcare technology conference to share my story and illuminate the ePatient perspective for the physicians, software developers and policy makers in the room. My husband, a well-known physician and healthcare informatician (a fancy word for data wonk), often conveyed my cancer story during meetings and conferences. As a result, many people in the field already knew a part of my tale.

To combat my fear, I leaned on God and leapt at the opportunity. As I checked my ego and let God's words spill out, His messages deepened the impact of the colorful, visual presentation I had created to share my cancer journey. The audience warmly embraced my story. Soon after, a media maven at the event videotaped an impromptu interview (conducted by my husband) as I shared my ePatient perspective. That video quickly circulated online and I found myself being cited on Twitter, Facebook and LinkedIn.

Since June 2013, I have been blessed to speak at over a dozen healthcare events, share my story in a follow up video interview, and was a featured guest on an internet radio show. The impact of my story and my ePatient advocacy efforts provided the opportunity to chair and form a new council centered on patient experience, in conjunction with a highly-esteemed industry leading association. Intimidated by the prospects of forming and leading an organization, I leaned on God for guidance and (again) leapt at the chance. In following God's lead, I invited a colleague who has lived the eFamily caregiver experience to act as co-chair (a bonus fourth leadership Rx: do what is best for the greater good, not just what is best for you).

In February 2014, with support of our partner association, we launched The Patient Experience Council affiliated with the Louis Sullivan Institute for Healthcare Innovation. Today, we enjoy the privilege of working with a team of brilliant and reputable ePatients and eFamily Caregivers, each hand-picked to help drive patient experience centered change across the healthcare system.

God continues to expand my leadership path by way of new projects, engagements and unfathomable recognition as one of fifteen Disruptive Women to Watch in 2015 (an honor I share with the Honorable Ruth Bader Ginsburg, Maria Shriver and a cadre of exceptionally successful women). This unexpected recognition is a testament to God and all the incredible people He called upon to help position me for this deeply humbling experience, given there are countless women more deserving of the award.

My fallible nature assures that I frequently stumble and fall on my path, while fear threatens to hijack my time, energy, focus, relationships and success. When I succumb to my failings and fears, my leadership journey is peppered with potholes. Leaning on God is my best insurance policy for leadership success. So as you think about how your life experiences, beliefs, fears and faith shape your view of the world, I hope this piece awakens your senses.

Your Turn, Your Story

Take a moment to consider the leadership role *you* can play as an ePatient. What can you do to seek out the medical care you need, prefer and desire for YOU? How can you do the same for your loved ones as an eFamily Caregiver? I hope that this brief personal journey I've shared inspires you to explore your own leadership story by taking a moment to consider the themes that resonate with your own life and faith journey. My final wish for you is to let go, listen, be heard, lean into your spiritual path and leap into leadership, even in the face of fear or judgment, so that you can inspire others through your authentic story.

Kym Martin is a three-time, 30-year cancer survivor who is passionate about enhancing the patient experience in healthcare. Kym endured three different cancer diagnoses through three distinct stages of life and chose three different cancer treatment paths. Kym is an ePatient and Co-Chair of the **Patient Experience Council**. She shares an insightful *video interview* with her multi-talented husband, Ross Martin, MD (a phenom in the world of healthcare technology and music). The video was filmed at Health Datapalooza in 2013.

Kym is a humbled honoree of the distinction, **Disruptive Women to Watch in 2015**, recognized along with the Hon. Ruth Bader Ginsburg, Maria Shriver and a dozen other dynamic and highly-acclaimed female leaders. http://www.kymmartin.com/

Story Eighteen

Uncharted Territory:
Pioneering Women's Football

Donna Wilkinson

There's nothing typical about a woman who chooses her armor for battle, puts on her helmet and shoulder pads, and hears the click-clack, click-clack of cleats as she walks through the tunnel into the hallowed grounds of a football stadium. She makes her way to the field and prepares for battle. This one has accepted a different kind of mission. She will fling her body around with reckless abandon putting her life and limb on the line to pursue a passion deep within her. She is doing something she was told she could never do, having an experience previously exclusive to men.

The life of a female warrior may not be as glorious as that of her male counterparts, but those who discover the life she lives look with amazement at what she has accomplished. The women who play American tackle football are breaking gender barriers and changing paradigms. Playing a male dominated sport as a woman is liberating and empowering at many levels.

Women's football has grown over the past 15 years in the United States to where nearly four thousand women play on 100 different teams, in three leagues. Women now play tackle football in more than a dozen countries around the world. As women break free from old paradigms and step onto a platform where physical presence and strength are requirements for success, they find their power and face their fears or the game eats them up. The female warriors who rise to the challenge have an ever growing passion for the game and a commitment to excellence that is only rivaled by the worlds best. Going into my 15th season with the DC Divas, I see the impact we are having on women around world and I'm honored to be one of the pioneers.

This is a series of reflections and part of my story from a little girl who dreamed of playing football to a two-time Gold Medal Winner for TEAM USA.

It's only a dream.

I was 5 years old when I declared to my family that I wanted to grow up to be big and strong like my grandfather so I could play football. My family thought it was cute and shrugged it off as a childish fantasy. Little did they know, I would grow up to be a leader in the women's football movement.

By junior high the boys in my neighborhood had joined the football team. I wanted to play so badly and this was when it hit me that I couldn't play because I was a girl. I was crushed and this challenged me at the deepest levels to prove myself as a woman and an athlete. I locked into an aggressive, disciplined and focused approach and was successful playing multiple sports, bringing home league championships, MVP honors and a college scholarship. This took me right to the doorstep of women's football where my career began two years after graduating from college.

It was the hitting that drew me to the game, a place where I could demonstrate my strength and show the world how powerful I was as a woman.

During the early part of my career, my masculine energy coupled with a big ego that needed to win ruled me. That aggressive and dominant energy seemed to be a perfect fit for football. I was results driven, loved everything about the game, and was willing to give all of myself to the sport. I practiced hard and let out my inner beast on the field as the nickname "the Animal" emerged and became my alter-ego. Off the field, I focused on the training, nutrition and healing modalities that would give me the edge.

Winning was always a motivating force and the reason why I put so much time into preparation and training. Winning is how we are taught to measure success, but it was deeper than that. Losing burned me energetically like fire running through my veins. The burning was about perfection. I had to get it right or it would torment me Winning made me feel good and aligned with Who I Am, and losing created a whole new experience that eventually reached a boiling point.

I began to set records and have individual success on the field. I was recognized and celebrated, but still longed for a championship. It was after a playoff game that we felt we should have won, that my attachment to winning could be seen for its true nature. A few players gathered in the basement of the sports pub to watch game film. As the game went on and we saw the mistakes that led to our demise, frustration began to build among the players. A few of us went upstairs to the ladies room, and the energy erupted. A teammate and I exchanged punches and I threw her up against the wall in the back of the stall. The other players began punching each other and "fight club" was in full swing. We all loved each other and the only way we knew how to express our pain and love at that moment was by beating each other up. Fight Club continued until our quarterback emerged with a bloody nose dripping onto her white t-shirt. We began to laugh at the absurdity of it all and calmed ourselves enough to leave that space and move on. We took our beat up hearts and bodies to one of the players' apartments where we submerged ourselves in our pain for the next week. Then it was back to preparing for the next season. This experience opened my eyes to the inherent weakness of identifying with external results.

I've always felt a deep sense that I am here to bring something special into the world. I had it all – a loving family, good education, athletic talent, opportunity to express myself, a promising football career, and my parents religion. So what was I fighting inside? Why did I feel like I had to prove myself over and over again? Was I missing something? I didn't know, so I kept on fighting... fighting to be the best, fighting to be right, fighting to be at the top. I experienced constant duality, and the football field was the perfect place to play out the drama.

The battle continued until I was jolted into a new reality.

It was sudden and took my breath away. The day I got the call that my mom had a heart attack and was in the hospital is as vivid as if it happened yesterday. Two days later she passed away at the age of 58. My mom lived in perfect alignment with her religious beliefs and healthy living principles. She was my example of how to do things right, and her death forced me to question what she might have missed in her extensive study and care. It created a deep longing and then depression.

Fortunately, I had the team to lean on for support. The field was a place where I could get out of the pain for several hours, and feel alive and inspired again. But this season would bring a new challenge, and push me to another level. I was making a tackle along the sideline when I felt a pop in my knee. I knew it was bad as I was carted off to the locker room with a torn ACL. I elected to wait until after the season was over to have knee surgery so I could rehab and potentially play in a playoff game. This was the best team we had put together in our six-year history and we had high expectations. I went to physical therapy and trained every day through the playoffs. We continued to win and made it to the Championship game. I had worked so hard to get to that point that I couldn't let the moment pass me by. I came in for a few plays, picked up a first down and scored a two-point conversion to contribute to the victory. It was a personal victory and our first National Championship title. I celebrated for a month, then it was time for surgery.

After surgery I was left to face myself. Additional damage done to my knee by playing on it torn put me in a position of limited mobility for three months. It had been nearly a year since my mom had passed and without a physical outlet to release the energy, I became depressed. If my mom lived a healthy life in alignment with the highest example of her beliefs, how could she have died so young? How could I feel so disconnected from what she taught me after following in her footsteps my whole life? Why was my life a battle? I needed a change of perspective and a new way of looking at things. I got to the point of giving up control. I couldn't go on if things were the same. Right there I made a decision to find healing, and release everything else. I let go completely to allow myself the space to find some answers.

From that position I was able to receive what I couldn't when I was fighting everything. A therapist guided me to look within. People, books and information began to appear. With the time I had to be off my feet, I began to consume as much as possible every day. I wanted to know why life was the way it was, and I needed to know how things really worked as they were no longer working for me.

I looked within and found the Source of all creation.

The coming days and months were powerfully moving as I opened my mind to new ideas. I read and listened to authors that presented leading edge information on consciousness, spirituality, science and the quantum field. One by one these new ideas about life were evaluated and taken within for further contemplation. New answers brought up new questions. I opened pandora's box. Everything was shifting and unstable. I had to take the information within and process it, then go through my own personal experience of living the new awareness. I released many deeply held beliefs that were no longer serving me, and made space for the new ideas to grow. The process of evaluating and looking at everything was extensive. This was one of the most exciting and at the same time most challenging times of my life. I added Bikram yoga and meditation to my regular training schedule and that helped me ground myself and go deeper.

I found my true power when I accepted myself as a creator, and a co-creator of life. I discovered that every thought is creative and has the power of prayer. There is no judge out there saying yes to some and no to others, but rather there is a creative process that has been unfolding since before the beginning of time. The natural laws that govern the Universe extend to all creation and are consistent to all.

This was a new picture of life that wasn't centered around a battle. It was a creative place where all internal thoughts have a reflection in the external world. I became aware of the important role that all levels of emotion (including anger) play in the healing response. I began moving up the emotional guidance scale one emotion at a time. I accepted responsibility for the things I had attracted into my experience. A feeling of genuine power began to emerge from beyond my ego. It was not dependent on others or anything external. It was a space within that allowed my sense of Self to expand and connect to ALL.

On the field my new sense of connection extended to everyone including teammates and competitors.

With a new sense of connection to myself, and all of life, things began to change on the field. I was no longer competing to prove myself, and my sense of self worth was no longer tied to winning. The game became a space where my new creative reality could play out. I didn't need fight club anymore. My leadership style shifted from a masculine dominating style, to a more balanced approach that leads from the heart. I still put every ounce of who I am into every play, but now I'm not playing with pain and anger as a motivating force. I work to find that place of alignment and balance between the aggression of football and the peace in my heart. It's an interesting swing back and forth that challenges me at different turns. I'm motivated to keep growing and push the boundaries of what is mentally and physically possible to do on the field.

ONE Team - Mission GOLD!

As I emerge from the locker room with my uniform fitted to perfection, I feel like a superhero. In this state I am ageless in a moment. It's the feel of the gloves fit snug to my fingers and the press of the fabric against my sculpted body under the shoulder pads. It's the rush of energy that flows through me as I merge into the moment, one with everything around me. This is my sanctuary, this is my paradise, the world disappears and everything slows down. I've found a moment that takes me deep into myself.

It gives me the chills to hear the click-clack of cleats hit the concrete as I walk through the tunnel of these hallowed grounds. I am playing America's sport, and representing the United States of America in the game that we all love. After a decade of playing in the women's tackle league in the USA, I was selected to join a special group of women who made history playing in the first ever IFAF Women's World Championships of tackle football in Stockholm, Sweden. Our role as pioneers, leaders and elite players in the sport of women's football brought us together for this moment as "ONE Team ONE Mission". We are to be ambassadors for the sport of women's football and here to win a Gold Medal for Team USA.

As 45 of the top players from across the US came together for this mission, we all put our egos aside and took on the idea of representing our country and putting USA first. We bonded faster than any other team I have ever been a part of. One of the reasons we came together so fast was because of "The ONION" which is coach Mac's creation. Coach Mac was a beautiful soul who put together a team bonding activity in which we were layered together like an onion and were taken through a visualization experience with guided meditation. Mac took us through each situation and prepared us to navigate the environment we would be in one step at a time. During the mini-camp we created a sisterhood of love and connection that will last a lifetime. We visualized each moment together as a team and banded together to make history. We were encouraged to write in our journals and soak in every moment.

It was an intense football experience with three games in seven days for the chance to be called World Champions. We breezed through our first two games versus Finland and Austria and played a more veteran Canadian team (who beat Germany and Sweden) for the championship. Team USA dominated every facet of the game and made our mark on history shutting out the competition, and winning the first gold medal in International women's tackle football competition.

It's been powerful to see the growth of women's football around the world. Team USA set an example for how the game should be played and the world responded. I was one of several women who came back in 2013 as a member of Team USA to play in the second World Championships in Finland. Winning the gold created a high so powerful that I found myself chasing that feeling after we returned home. Those feelings are impossible to match in everyday life and it reminded me again to go within and become grounded. The cycle of flow took me back to an external focus and reminded me that the process of growth is fluid and will keep presenting me with the lessons I'm here to learn. I am reminded that I can't chase it. I simply have to be it.

"The last place I was expecting to have a self-reflecting mirror show me everything about myself is on the football field."

But a mirror is exactly what you get when you play a sport where your thoughts, fears and doubts play out in a physical and dangerous game. A momentary distraction or hesitation and you drop the pass, miss the tackle, or get blown up... Do you release that mistake from your mind and focus back on the next play with more confidence and determination then on the previous play? ...Or do you identify with the mistake and start to believe that you drop passes and don't have good hands, that you can't make the play? Either way, you will start a creative process that will solidify in your experience the belief you have about yourself.

This has been a hall of mirrors and I have had to re-create myself over and over again. Every year there has been a new opportunity and some kind of challenge to grow from. From these mirrors I have come to know myself, and am conscious of the world I am creating and co-creating with everyone around me.

Donna Wilkinson is a 15 year veteran of the DC Divas and two-time Gold Medalist in women's tackle football. To maintain peak performance and recover from injuries she integrates leading edge health technologies with natural healing modalities for extraordinary results. Donna has degrees in Health Fitness Management and Business Administration and utilizes the latest advancements in cellular rejuvenation in her holistic health practice. She is a global leader and speaker dedicated to raising consciousness, health education, the empowerment of women and developing leaders. She lives in the moment with inspiration, passion, integrity, alignment and expansion.

Website: www.donnawilkinson.net Business:

www.teamasea.com/molecularwellness Twitter: @donnawilk33

Story Nineteen

Answering a Calling:
The Heal My Voice Story

Andrea Hylen

God does not call the qualified. God qualifies the called.
~Michael Bernard Beckwith

The bridge across the highway was trembling from cars driving by as I walked on the sidewalk towards Toluca Lake, CA. The sun was warm and shining on this December afternoon as I daydreamed with God. The Forty-four (44) BlogTalk radio shows I was hosting on grief transformation were in process; 44 shows in 45 days over the holidays of Thanksgiving, Hanukkah, Christmas, New Year's Eve and ending with Epiphany. With each show, I felt my voice growing stronger as I talked about a journey with grief, sharing feelings and tools for healing the loss of a brother, a son, a husband, a home, a job, and a life threatening illness. While celebrations of joy and laughter were happening in many households over the holidays, I was holding a space for loss and grief.

Lately, my afternoon walk and conversations with God had been about the radio shows. My flip chart of 44 days was now full and the shows were in flow. Today I had other questions for God. I had been living in California for eleven months. I loved it and at the same time I was frustrated. I was still waiting for a message with a higher purpose. Why had I experienced the calling to leave my community in Baltimore? Why am I here? How am I to serve? What can I do to make money and support my daughter, Hannah, and me? What is the next step after this immersion in writing and speaking about grief?

I heard the whisper of words in the background of my mind. I might have brushed them away as a thought passing through except for one thing. I could feel my heart beat faster, my lungs suddenly filled with air and tears filled my eyes. The words, "Heal My Voice," were more than a whisper. They were filling me with emotion. Heal My Voice was mixed with the unheard voices of women. I could feel the power of their voices; their ideas, thoughts, dreams and feelings that had been stuffed down by trauma, loss, grief, diminishment, abandonment, and feelings of less than, and "too muchness." Heal My Voice was calling me to create something; a program, a business that could serve the voices of women. To heal, reclaim power and step into greater leadership in their lives at the dinner table, the community and in the world.

I can still feel the power of that moment. It is almost 4 years later and I still get teary, my heart beating faster with chills running up and down my body when I hear the words, "Heal My Voice." We now have six completed books with 120 stories in Heal My Voice, a non-profit tax exempt organization that has served the everyday, extraordinary, entrepreneurial woman; Two books from Heal My Voice Sweden with forty stories written in Swedish in programs led by Marie Ek Lipanovska. There have been two additional programs: a letter-writing program between women who reside in prison and women who reside in the free world and a writing circle for women in a residential addiction recovery program.

When "Heal My Voice" appeared I had undergone a "life preparation." All had been the foundation that would prepare me for holding a space of energy and words of compassion and understanding as each woman wrote her story.

I wrote this blog in January 2010 after leaving Maryland:

Finally on the road and headed to Columbus, Ohio for the first night's sleep, Five years ago, Hurley, my husband was dying from cancer. Everything in our lives stopped. He died nine months later. For the last five years I have been releasing material possessions, businesses, a house and the dreams we had together.

As I drove away from Baltimore today, it was hard to believe that we were finally on our way to California. A year of talking and planning with my 17 year old daughter, Hannah, and now here it is.

It is hard to connect with the realness, the significance of this moment. It feels surreal.

This morning I told myself, drive, just drive. This is the spiritual practice of the week. Drive. Observe nature, the bumper stickers and vanity license plates. Let the feelings wash over you and drive. No thinking or figuring anything out. Let the last five years and all of the moments it took to get here, just BE. Let everything settle. Listen to your heart. This is the first day of a new chapter.

Hello World! I AM Andrea.

I arrived in California five days later with the expectancy that the answers would be there. After all, I had prepared for years, right? My husband died in 2005. Now it was Jan 2010. I spent two years of time clearing out my husband's business. Another year of clearing out the basement of our house and his unfinished projects. I had grieved. Quietly. Silently. Loudly. I had done the deep, personal growth work. Found my way through the maze of grief. And now, arriving in California, wouldn't God have a message for me? A note by the side of the bed? A voice mail? Something that showed me the next step to take in creating a new life? A job? An apt? A community?

After a week of not knowing what was next, the message did come. It just wasn't what I was expecting. I heard God say: Release more.

What? God, are you crazy? What else do I have to release? I sold my house. Sold or gave away most of my belongings. Moved away from my community. Let go of all of the roles I felt gave me value. RELEASE MORE? What more do I have to release?

Then, I heard it. Release all the voices of the people I cared about the most. Release them from my mind. Release the "shoulds" and the "coulds." Release their expectations. Stop playing their voices in my head every time I take a step. Stop listening for their approval, and the ideas of what a life should look like for a woman who was 53 years old. Follow a new path. Empty myself. Look for the signs along the way. Listen to my own voice. Say yes.

And that is what I did. I started with baby steps. One day I heard *go for a walk.* Fifteen minutes later... *Now, go back to the hotel, get your computer and go to the coffee shop.* I started to write a blog and there was a "ding" from the computer as an email from James Twyman arrived about "The Next Top Spiritual Author" contest. I signed up and began a 3-month journey of writing, exploring video, asking for votes on Facebook. Structure. Focused intention. Learning.

That was the beginning. It took me 10 months to really hear my voice without also hearing the voice of my father, mother, sister, brother or friends. It took me 10 months to feel clear enough to hear new ideas and messages without thinking about how my choices would affect or hurt a family member.

During the 10 months, I let go of weekly phone calls with my sister. I let go of the daily safety net of friends. I learned to live without all of the identities that gave me "value." Girl Scout Leader. Homeschooling Mom. Maryland Resident. Wife of Hurley. Mother of Cooper. In my new location, I was just a woman sitting in the corner of the coffee shop writing every morning. No one saw "my value, my wisdom" just by looking at me.

For someone who had longed for community all her life and finally found a "home" in Baltimore, the idea of spending so much time alone was torture at times. Standing by the ocean in California with no family, no friends, no community when at the center of my being, connection with people was the most important part of my life. It didn't seem logical at the time. Now I know why I needed to do it.

Looking back, I can't imagine leading Heal My Voice without that time alone. I cultivated trust in myself and in God. I cultivated trust in my intuition and the inner guidance that comes from sitting in stillness, crying on my knees at the beach, shaking my fists at the sky and yelling at God. There is a rich, fertile field that I can access now.

Another moment in April 2011. I had been asking God to show me the group of women I would connect with to launch the first Heal My Voice program. I was walking home from Priscilla's, my morning coffee shop writing location. I received the "download" of inspired action. Go to the Awesome Women Hub Event in Baltimore. Post on Facebook. Reach out to your community. Get support and go. Now!

I quickened my walking pace to get back to the apartment. Within 24 hours, I had received donations in the form of a free flight, a ticket to the event, a place to stay, a fundraising event idea and a bottle of Abundance Shampoo.

I had stayed connected with people on Facebook. I had grown connections during that 10 months: celebrated women, and shared deep feelings. I said yes to supporting the Awesome Women Hub event in California. I had been laying a foundation that was ready to receive me. When it was time to reconnect with the world again, I needed help and support. There would be no Heal My Voice, if I hadn't had a community of supporters. The program price for that first year was $100 per person. Weekly phone calls, individual coaching, writing and editing support, radio shows and social media. Some of the women became sponsors for the book with larger donations or media coverage. It was the friends who believed in me, used frequent flyer miles to fly me back to Baltimore, who picked me up at the airport, gave me shelter and food, drove me to networking meetings, encouraged me when I got emotionally whacked by, believe it or not, women who criticized me. I needed help. The community of support from the believers helped me to practice listening within and take inspired action.

I have learned to wait and listen and understand that everything has it's own timing. This is the 6th Book Project in 3 years. Each book has required more excavation of me. I have healed a part of my own life story in each project. I have reclaimed more of my essence and cultivated my own personal power one step ahead of the women I lead.

It is now August 2014. A few months ago, I received another piece of guidance. Put my personal belongings back into the 10 x 10 storage unit in California. Pack a suitcase and a backpack and live on the road for a year. This time it is with deeper intention to connect with women and communities around the world. To have conversations, listen to their voices, follow the guidance from within and discover what is next for me and for Heal My Voice.

After 3 months of living on the road in Santa Barbara, Santa Cruz, Baltimore, and New York City, I am now in Malmo, Sweden with Marie Ek Lipanovska, the founder of Heal My Voice Sweden and with the women who have written stories in Swedish. At an Open House last week, one of the women entered the room with her newborn baby and husband. The community gathered around her in celebration of this new life, a new voice. As she was leaving, she thanked me for following this vision. She invited me to look around and see the women and see what is being created by women joining in community and sharing their vulnerable, powerful voices with each other and through their stories in each book.

As I finished writing this story in Sweden, I received an email from the Facebook App, "A Message from God":

Today, Andrea, we believe God wants you to know that ...nothing is exciting if you know what the outcome is going to be. You keep wanting to know how things will play out, keep asking to see the future. God doesn't give anyone the power to know the future because life becomes maddeningly boring when you know everything upfront. So, instead of struggling, enjoy the uncertainty. To be alive means to not know.

We all receive intuitive information every day. Our body gives us clues about the amount of exercise, rest, touch, and food it needs for nourishment. Our soul gives us clues about what it wants for growth. Moment by moment we say yes or no. We use the information or we don't.

Then there is the deeper calling. The one that calls for you to surrender to life, to follow the inspiration step by step, to let go and release your comfort zone, to crack open something new in you so that a fuller expression can emerge. It will require a deeper level of commitment to grow and a radical amount of self-love.

Take a moment now. What is the story you are ready to write?

Shhhh...listen...it is calling you from within. Pick up the pen, the notebook, or the computer and start writing.

Your Voice Matters.

Andrea Hylen believes in the power of a woman's voice to usher in a new world. She is the founder of Heal My Voice, a Minister of Spiritual Peacemaking, a Writing and Transition Coach and Orgasmic Meditation teacher. Andrea has discovered her unique gifts while parenting three daughters and learning to live life fully after the deaths of her brother, son and husband. She is currently living out of a suitcase following her intuition as she collaborates with women and men in organizations and travels around the world speaking, teaching and leading workshops. Her passion is authentically living life and supporting others in doing the same. To connect with Andrea and learn about current projects go to: *www.andreahylen.com and **www.healmyvoice.org**.*

Heal My Voice Projects

www.healmyvoice.org

Join us in our mission to help each woman discover her voice:

Heal My Voice empowers and supports women and girls globally to heal, reclaim their voice and step into greater leadership in their lives and in the world.

Your Voice Matters!

TO ORDER additional copies of this book and to discover additional Heal My Voice books in this series and current programs, go to the Heal My Voice website:

www.HealMyVoice.org

Thank you

to our

Sponsors

Sponsors

Mary K. Baxter
http://dramaticadventure.com/

Cassandra Herbert
http://www.justbeewellness.com/

Ellen Koronet
http://lnkcreative.com/

Marie Ek Lipanovska
http://www.healmyvoicesweden.com/

Monisha Mittal
http://www.yourinnerease.com/

Karen Porter
http://www.mamaporter.com/

Amber Scott
http://trueuvoice.com/

Jamie Dee Schiffer
http://www.a-passionate-life.com/

Beth Terrence
http://www.bethterrence.com/

Kathleen Nelson Troyer
http://gentlymovingforward.net/

Heal My Voice Book Series

Fearless Voices:
True Stories by Courageous Women

Empowered Voices:
True Stories by Awakened Women

Inspired Voices:
True Stories by Visionary Women

Harmonic Voices:
True Stories by Women on the Path to Peace

Tender Voices:
True Stories by Women on a Journey of Love

Feminine Voices:
True Stories by Women Transforming
Leadership